Through Rose Colored Glasses

Donna Deegan

Closet Books
Jacksonville

Dust jacket design by Oscar Senn
Cover photo courtesy Paul King
Back cover photo courtesy Donna Deegan

1st Edition
First Printing
October 2009

ISBN 1-891-23219-0

This book is in no way a representation of Medical fact or Medical
Procedure. It is for information only, and should not be considered
as medical advice. Please consult with your health practitioner
before considering any therapy or therapy protocol.

Grateful acknowledgment is made to the following for permission to reprint excerpts
from previously published material:

Hodder & Stoughton for permission to use excerpts from
The Holy Longing: The Search for a Christian Spirituality
by Ronald Rolheiser, Doubleday, 1999.

Gerald G. Jamposky for permission to use excerpts from
Love is Letting Go of Fear by Gerald G. Jamposky
Celestial Arts an imprint of Ten Speed Press, 1975 & 1999.

Closet Books
PO Box 440504
Jacksonville, FL 32222

www.ClosetBooks.com

Printed in the United States of America
2468097531

For Susan Mehrlust and all the "Susans"
who show us the truth of life.
Love is the cure for all that ails us. ♥

Contents

Foreword

Runners always seem to make the best friends. Calling Donna Deegan a dear friend of mine, after meeting her at The National Marathon to Fight Breast Cancer in January of 2008, is no exception.

It took me no time at all after our initial introduction in Jacksonville Beach, Florida to realize that Donna and I shared a similar passion for running and all of its offerings. I came to see Donna first as a fellow runner and then as a breast cancer survivor. Her gratitude for all of the good that came to her through running, far outweighed the challenges she confronted as a breast cancer patient.

It was as if she immediately recognized that both surviving breast cancer and running, specifically marathoning, are challenges to embrace and enjoy. Both demand a certain mind set and understanding of goal setting and perseverance.

However, breast cancer can be beat or "finished" as Donna would say, but with marathoning there is always another finish line to cross with new goals and aspirations.

By founding The National Marathon to Fight Breast Cancer, Donna has instilled hope in thousands of women and men, (many of whom are breast cancer survivors) to summon the "Can Do" spirit in themselves and others by looking at the roads ahead as avenues for opportunity, healing and healthy living.

Good health and healing seem to take place when one can be at peace and relaxed. Balancing ones interests as they relate to the mind, body and spirit can lead to an inner sense of peace. When an individual is able to strike a balance in the life she leads, goals seem to be easier to achieve and life becomes more meaningful, enjoyable and fulfilling. Just as Donna has found a similar balance of the mind body and spirit to work positively in her life, I have found this balance to work in similar ways as I try to balance my life as a mother, wife, involved citizen in the community and in the sport of running.

Donna has founded and fashioned an event that will undoubtedly help to one day find a finish line for breast cancer while enriching and improving the lives of breast cancer patients, their families, friends and runners of all abilities.

I thank Donna for her friendship, courage, joie d'vie, passion for our sport and for her desire to help others help themselves by always putting one foot in front of the other and never looking back in fear.

It is my hope, that with what she started in founding the National Marathon to Fight Breast Cancer, and in light of the current health care crisis, physical activity (running and walking) will one day become part of every patient's recovery protocol.

Run on for miles to come in good health.

With great admiration,
Joan Benoit Samuelson

Through Rose Colored Glasses

Donna Deegan

Closet Books

Jacksonville

Introduction

Mark 5:36
Fear Not; Only Believe

In 2008 I founded The National Marathon to Fight Breast Cancer. So my next statement may sound a bit strange.

I have come to believe cancer should not be viewed as a fight. I think the focus on fighting just gives the disease its energy, its persistence in our lives. This was not an easy lesson for me. I'm as competitive as people come. I'm a journalist after all. I thrive on deadlines, making things happen. I'm crazy about winning. So am I suggesting we give up? Not at all.

In this book I'll do my best to explain. My life as a journalist has taught me that the search for the truth requires an open mind and the willingness to listen and learn. At the age of 48, I'm happy to say I am still learning. As the saying goes, the teacher is heard when the student is ready. This revelation came after my third diagnosis with the disease. For five years I was cancer free. On the fifth anniversary of my "all clear" I was ready to party. I was deep into preparing for our inaugural race, and planning to argue my case for a longer absence from the Mayo Clinic needle patrol, when a small spot in my left lung sent me back to square one.

Square one is a good place to start when looking for the truth. Any cancer patient who has done double duty or more on this disease will tell you the thoughts run rampant. What did I do to bring this back? Am I eating something, breathing something, did I forget to go to confession last month? After that, our instincts tell us to swing away. Get immediately into battle mode. Prepare for the fight.

In *The Good Fight*, I offered that I have spent much of my life waiting for the other shoe to drop. When I was too happy for too long that little voice of dread would always creep in. "OK, things are going too well, time for something bad to happen." It was my means of protection. Really very responsible, I thought. I would create these movies in my head of every possible bad outcome and then feel good that at least I was prepared for the worst, should the worst come.

I'd have told you then that I was mostly a happy person. I see now though, that despite great support, inside of me I was still too ready to view the world through a lens of fear. What I continue to learn is that it is fear that keeps us imprisoned by cancer and impedes our healing. It is only in letting go of that fear that we are finally free to live.

Every time I have dealt with cancer it has moved me forward. It has prompted me to look more deeply inside myself than I ever would have looked, especially at such a relatively young age. It has brought the most wonderful teachers into my life and it has ultimately taught me to view the world through a new lens. A lens of love.

This all may sound a bit esoteric, but it was always there, hiding in plain sight. Now I can see all the steps on the path that have led me to this conclusion. When it comes to cancer, we need to take a make love not war mentality.

Do I believe we can find a cure for breast cancer? Of course I do. I believe our marathon and the brilliant researchers we fund are right on the cusp of a cure and I believe I am going to be around to announce they've found it. I also believe no cure can be complete unless it continues on the inside. Doctors can find a miracle drug, but for health to be sustained, we cannot constantly be 'at war' in our minds. The mind, body and spirit must all play a role.

We are a society that thrives on the thrill of victory. Me included. In a race, that's great. It's fun. When it comes to cancer, placing ourselves in perpetual fight mode only wears us out. The concept of beating cancer may make us feel courageous. But how many times have we seen cancer beaten back, only to return with a vengeance? We need to connect the dots. A love revolution makes a lot more sense.

As you'll read in these pages, the day of our inaugural race was a perfect example. There was grace in the air. The joy on that day was palpable. I received literally thousands of letters from people who felt the same thing.

Most significantly, with study and practice, I have learned ways to sustain that joy in my everyday life. Those days when I don't have a crowd of thousands to carry me.

It's funny. For years, I've been running in pink sunglasses with rose colored lenses. But in a true sense I am seeing the world through those rose colored glasses for the first time and life is so good.

I hope to share the view.

Acknowledgements

So many people have made this book possible. I want to begin by thanking my book editor and dear friend Lynn Skapyak Harlin. This is our second book project together and I couldn't ask for a more loving committed guide. Thanks to George Gilpatrick, publisher of Closet Books, for his continued faith in me. I'm grateful to Paul King for his beautiful work on the cover photo, and to Oscar Senn for his artistry on the cover and in the pages of this book.

Thanks to my colleagues at First Coast News for giving me the flexibility to make this book a reality. I'm indebted to the board and staff of 26.2 with Donna and The Donna Foundation for their unflinching support and tireless work to bring a world class marathon to Jacksonville Beach. To all of the sponsors, runners and walkers who make the trek to help us finish breast cancer and care for those living with the disease, I will never be able to adequately express my gratitude. We are making a difference with every step.

And a most special thanks to my very patient and loving family, my husband Tim and my children Danielle and Drew. I love you all beyond words.

The roar that lies on the other side of silence

The forest fire, that is fear so deny it

U2
Breathe
From the album
No Line On The Horizon

1 | *Running* to Stand Still

September 12, 2007

I want to move. Get to a destination.

A lot of people like to run on treadmills. It's efficient, I suppose, but it's not for me. If I lived, in say, Woodbury, Minnesota or points north, I could see that running in three feet of snow might be a disincentive. Beyond that, running on a flat piece of rubber that spins around and around , enclosed by rails, staring at a bunch of flashing red numbers and going nowhere? It is literally running to stand still. Sort of like a hamster.

Even if I've done the same run hundreds of times, and I have, it's always different. It's like taking a trip with an old friend and watching that relationship deepen. The more I give the more I get. No matter what kind of day I've had, or how many deadlines I face, regardless of how confining my circumstances may seem, I can lace up my running shoes, hit the road and go as far as my legs and my will can take me.

My favorite runs are in the early morning through the beaches I've known and loved all my life. I leave home and head north on 1st Street, passing through the palm lined streets of Jacksonville Beach. A quaint A-frame church, with a tall white steeple, marks the transition to Neptune

Beach. Harriet Pruette is on her daily walk. Wild colored socks and all. The locals call her The Queen of Vice for all her years as Vice Mayor of the small seaside community.

As I close in on Atlantic Beach, my nose catches the breakfast smells coming from Shelby's Coffee Shop and the scent of stale beer that wafts from Pete's Bar. I hit the red bricks that signal the entrance to "The Corner," the name given to the popular restaurants and clubs that serve as the welcome center to our northern beaches. Other runners are gathering to start their morning. All the time the ocean is there to my right giving me glimpses of white water and sparkles.

Kids on bikes and skateboards whiz by as the road narrows into Beach Avenue. Wood shingled houses sport names like "Hi Tide" and there is a big oceanfront yard with a gazebo that looks like a magazine cover. I'm already anticipating Bull Park. My perfectly placed water stop. A small white cottage faces the southeast corner. It's used for weddings, acoustic concerts and the occasional meeting. The water fountain is exactly two and a half miles into my run and always a welcome sight.

From there it's deep into Atlantic Beach where no house resembles the next. There is one home that reminds me of the tree house in the movie, Swiss Family Robinson and when I pass it I make my secret wish to live there. I have the whole fantasy played out in my head. Someone calls and says this is your lucky day! If you can give me the exact address of the home of your dreams, it's yours. I know the address by heart, of course, and repeat it immediately.

"The hill" at 19th Street gives the only hint of a challenge for the day. At the top a house that is built entirely underground peeks out of the grass.

I race down the backside and George Mayforth, a competitive triathlete, is peddling south on his morning ride. We exchange hellos, and he makes a slow graceful wave with his left arm like a giant bird flying on the wind currents. I mirror the motion back to him with both arms. Our unspoken signal that we are both in full flight.

Just before I get to 20th Street I glance up at an elegant home that looks as if it was taken directly from a hill in Tuscany. Then it's a left on 20th a quick jog down Seminole Road past Susan Mehrlust's house and I disappear into the shade of Ocean Walk. It almost has a jungle feel. A different world from the one I left across the street. Moss hangs from clusters of enormous live oak trees and the philodendron plants are three times my size. The road rolls gently and the jasmine hangs so thick in the air it's intoxicating.

Mile five and it's time to turn for home. The beach is calling. I trace my steps back to the top of 19th and take the path down to the shore to the firm flat sands that carpet my way home. I like to run as close to the water as possible. On the outgoing tide there are glossy spots where the water reflects the sky. It looks as if someone has taken scissors and cut a patch out of the blue and the puffy white clouds and pasted them on the sand.

There is nothing like running in the clouds.

I fill my lungs with salt air, fix my eyes on the pelicans skimming the blue green waves and I am one of them. I could fly forever.

It's as far from a hamster's life as I can imagine. And I can imagine.

2 | The Hamster

September 12, 2007

Up two hours earlier than usual. I'm not going to run today, even though it would probably settle my mind. It's my system. On the day of my follow up tests I never run. What if it skews my numbers? Plus, I know I don't have to fast for these blood tests, but I do anyway. So eating and drinking are out. What if I eat something that makes my marker go up or does something funky to my liver enzymes? Why give my doctor reasons to worry?

My brain is doing the hamster. It is running its endless circles of fear. I tell myself I'm calm but the dull throbbing in the bottom of my gut knows different. It has been five years since my last chemo treatment for round number two with breast cancer. October 31, 2002 seems like a lifetime ago, and like yesterday. Despite a few hiccups that turned out to be nothing, I have had great results. Still the pre-test panic always creeps in. Damn, I'm weak. Why can't I just take these things in stride?

I go through the chorus in my head, "It is what it is, Donna. You can't change things with worry. Be calm."

Susan's pleas to go with the flow try to penetrate my brain. My dear friend and mentor died from breast cancer last year. The day she was diagnosed, the oncologist told her the news was grave. The cancer had spread. He gave her six months. She told him she didn't think so. Susan lived for more than ten years and to this day the doctors have no idea how. Her mantra was 'Each Day Is a Gift' and she lived life completely in the moment. She was the most joyful, grace-filled person I have ever met. Her circumstances didn't mean a thing. She was simply in love with life and everything about it.

"Don't let the cancer live you," she always told me. "Stop looking over your shoulder, and live."

I loved her spirit. Still do. It's a peace I cannot understand.

I start going through a list of all the reasons I have to be confident about today's tests.

I'm training for the New York City Marathon for heaven's sake. I ran 18 miles two weekends ago. Could I do that if something was wrong? OK, I've been unusually tired. So what? It's been a long hot training season. I should be tired.

Then my mind lights on a conversation with my doctor Edith Perez from the week before. We had only run five miles.

I almost couldn't finish. I had to stop several times. Finally she spoke up.

"You seem pretty tired today," she said. Her tone was probing. Her dark eyebrows knit in a frown. "Are you getting enough sleep?"

Of course I'm not getting enough sleep. I never get enough sleep. Edith knows this. She never sleeps either. It is one of the things we understand about each other. Sleep is what other people do when they are OK with getting less done. People like us survive on caffeine. Thank God for

Starbucks' tall red-eye. Diet Coke is Edith's drug of choice.

"Oh just burning the candle at both ends and in the middle for good measure," I said.

I was getting up early to train for New York, spending my entire mornings planning our own marathon, then working until midnight at my anchor duties at the television station. And oh, by the way, raising two kids.

"What normal person wouldn't be tired?"

"Of course," she agreed.

I hate it when Edith answers with one or two words. I always feel responsible for filling in the two-hundred or so that I figure she isn't saying.

It's time to leave for Mayo Clinic.

I have already been around the beads on my rosary, sprinkled myself with holy water, touched my Mary scapular, and crossed my chest with oil that had been blessed in Medjugore. Why can't I get off the wheel? Stretch my legs, still my mind.

Maybe it's because of the milestone. Five years clear, while not the same exclamation point as it is with most other cancers, is an awfully good sign. If all goes well, I will be monitored only once a year instead of every six months. I can ease my life even further away from being a patient and continue my focus on advocacy. I am already a long way down that path.

In 2003, I started a foundation for women with breast cancer. It was specifically designed to fill a need that wasn't being met. The Donna Foundation was formed to provide for the critical needs of women as they face breast cancer. We pay for mortgages, and car payments, co-pays, and child care for underserved women so they can focus on getting better instead of on just getting by.

Then in 2006, in a move that I still consider the coup of the century, Edith and I were able to persuade the powers that be at Mayo Clinic to partner with my Foundation to form 26.2 With Donna The National Marathon to Fight Breast Cancer. Edith had often expressed concern about the drop in funding for breast cancer research, and I was always looking for ways to better fund our efforts for the underserved. I already had a local running club that ran other people's marathons to raise money for the Foundation. So this seemed like a logical next step.

I knew there was no marathon out there specific to breast cancer and through my club, I had a great relationship with 1972 Olympian and running coach Jeff Galloway. We turned out to be the perfect triumvirate. Jeff would train the runners and get the word out through his massive international coaching organization. Edith's credibility in the breast cancer community would help to persuade Mayo and put us in touch with the players we needed to get started, and I as a news anchor/ breast cancer survivor would supply the broadcast megaphone. It was an enormous undertaking, but one that I knew from day one would be a success. I can be a very confident person when it comes to making things happen. I wish I could translate that to my health.

I walk through the double glass doors that lead to the cafeteria at Mayo and right through the chatting breakfast crowd to the lab registration desk just on the other side. I never park in the garage anymore. That's what I did before. Anything I did before, I don't do now. It's all part of the routine.

The cheerful woman at the desk says good morning to me in the way you do with someone you see all the time. She has perfect teeth and the strap to her Mayo badge is covered with angel pins of every size and type.

"Well hello there, Miss Donna, and how are you today?"

"I'm awesome," I lie. "And you?"

"Very good, busy morning," she says. "Date of birth, please?"

As she always does, she apologizes for having to ask me the same question I have now been asked at least three million times on my trips to Mayo.

"It's just policy," she says, shaking her head.

"Of course, 2/28/61."

"Right again," she says.

"You're all checked in Donna, just have a seat in the waiting room and someone will be right out to take you back."

Such a nice woman. Just once I wish she'd say, "You know what, there's no need for you to be here today. We've decided you've had all the tests any one person should have to endure in a lifetime. You are just fine. Have a great life!"

I take my regular seat at the left front of the room. That's the door Mike Kurtz always comes out of to get me. He is my favorite blood letter. Mike always lets me run my vanishing veins under the warm water, and sticks me just one time for pay dirt every time. He is not one of those evil people who dig around in a patient's veins in the desperate and always failing attempt to find the vein that's rolled away. Oh no, Mike is a champion. He is also very discreet.

"Deegan, Donna," he almost whispers, as his head peers out from behind the lab door.

I am off the chair and through the door before anyone else even knows he is there.

Mike turns on the faucet to get the water heating and then grabs a butterfly needle. I don't get along well with big needles and I get along even less well with people who try to use them on me.

"Still just using the left hand, Donna?"

I'm not allowed to use the right one because that is the side where my lymph nodes were removed.

And my left arm has been used so much that it's toast. So the hand it is.

"That's all I've got Mike, maybe after this week I will get a pass to use the right one."

"What's this week?"

"Five years, cancer free baby!" Even as I say it, I think I have just ticked off the mythical Murphy so I internally start to back pedal.

Mike draws four tubes of blood and I say a prayer to each to behave.

"OK, that's the last of it," he says, withdrawing the needle and wrapping my hand in gauze.

"Good deal. If you did a good job here I may not see you for a year."

It takes a couple of hours for the blood work to process. The tumor marker takes a bit longer. Sometimes it takes the afternoon. Other times I won't get the results for a couple of days.

I head straight from the lab to the cafeteria to refill my veins with coffee and head up to the 8th floor for my appointment with Edith.

Shelly Brock, Edith's nurse examines me first. She listens to my lungs with her stethoscope and says what she says every time.

"Best lungs I'll hear all day."

I take pride in this. As a distance runner my blood pressure is perfect, my pulse is down around 50, and when they tell me to take a deep breath I draw it from my toes. Check, check and check.

Edith, comes in, takes a quick look at my hot off the presses test results and proclaims everything "beautiful". Well almost everything.

"There is a slight elevation in your liver enzymes, but we have seen this many times. Your liver seems to be very sensitive. Did you have a glass of wine, or take any unusual medicines over the last several days?"

Of course I hadn't, but now I am looking for reasons.

"Well, I had some wine Saturday night, but that was four days ago."

Three days is my cut off. I never have anything that I figure could mess with my tests three days out.

"This alone, is not concerning," Edith says. "Everything else looks A-OK."

"No marker yet, though," I say.

"Not yet. How's your energy?"

"I had a great run yesterday."

And this is actually true. It was only a few miles, but it had felt great.

Edith repeats the exam Shelly has already done. She always does this.

Then she checks my perpetually lumpy breasts, my underarms. She palpates around my liver, checks the lymph nodes around my neck and we're done.

"Everything looks great, Donna! You can get dressed and get going."

And I am feeling myself start to relax. I want to ask her about spacing out my tests, but I want to wait for the marker. No sense in tempting Murphy twice in one day.

"Call me when the marker comes in," I say, as I'm hugging her good bye.

"Will do," she says, giving me a squeeze. And I'm out of there.

It's a strange deal being good friends with my doctor. Things are always a bit uncomfortable around test time. Neither of us acts quite normal. We sort of tip toe around each other, until everything is done.

This marker business is the worst. We both know I freak about it. No matter how many times Edith cautions me not to hang on the number "because it's just not a perfect test," of course I do.

I can tell immediately in her voice what the news is going to be. If she has good news, which she has for a long time now, I get a cheerful message with the results. When the news has not been so good, I get the dreaded, "Hi Donna, this is Edith, can you call me?"

Heading to work the next day, I stop for gas and return to hear the tell tale beep of my phone. I hit the button for my messages and there is Edith. She sounds urgent.

I don't get the good news. I also don't get the "call me" message.

"Donna, this is Edith. (Pause) I need for you to come to the clinic for a CT scan. Your marker came back at 52. I have already set up a time for tomorrow. (Pause) This is just a precaution, OK?"

I am frozen in place. Sitting in the gas station parking lot, I feel the shot to my solar plexus.

My deep lungs can't seem to get breath. I don't dial Edith. I dial my husband Tim. My voice is shaking.

"Hola Mi Amore," he says, like someone who doesn't realize the earth is on a collision course with an asteroid.

I can barely get the words out. "My marker came back high. Edith has already booked me for a CT scan."

"OK, let's not presume the worst," he says. Tim's voice is as calm and soothing as always. It's like salve.

You've had weird numbers pop up before and they've turned out to be nothing."

"Exactly, but Edith always says let's wait a couple of weeks and retest. Why didn't she say that this time?"

"I think she's just trying to be thorough," Tim says. " But that would be a good question to ask her."

I don't want to ask her. Don't want to talk to her at all. I'm supposed to be celebrating my liberation. Damn it, I have a marathon to plan. I am too busy to deal with this invasion of my sanity.

"Take a deep breath Donna and whatever it is, we will deal with it, OK?"

"OK, I'm going to call her now. "

"I love you. Just keep breathing ."

Breathing. Sure. That's the goal. Keep breathing.

I dial and Edith picks up at the speed of light.

"This is not what I had in mind," I say, in an angrier tone than I intend.

"I know, but let's just make sure this is nothing." Her voice is flat and quiet.

"Why don't we just redo the test?"

"Because this is not just a couple of points high, then there are the liver enzymes, and besides I don't like how tired you've been."

Edith, like most good doctors, has a sixth sense. She knows when she smells trouble. She acts as much out of instinct as she does out of science.

I wish momentarily that she wasn't so good.

I want to go back to yesterday. To five minutes ago.

"It's just to make sure," she says again. There is nothing in her tone that sounds confident.

My brain goes into rewind. A past conversation just like this one flashes in my mind.

For the sake of sanity I place a wall between the fear in my heart and the words that come out of my mouth.

"I'll hold the party and the parade for one more day, but that's it."

"Sounds like a plan."

We hang up, I crank the car and I head off into a completely different day than the one I woke up to.

3 | *B*reathe Deep and Hold

September 13, 2007

Lying flat on the CT scanner. So cold my teeth are chattering. The nurse has kindly agreed to allow me to keep my clothes on. No designer grey robe and rubber bottomed socks today. That at least makes me feel more human. Tim is not allowed into the room with me. Once again I'm left alone with my radiation and my manic head. How many times have I done this? Sixty? Six-hundred? I hear the whir of the machine and a fuzzy voice floats through the speaker from behind the glass wall.

"Take a deep breath and hold." I am swallowed by the machine as it clicks and buzzes over me.

"And you can breathe," says the voice.

This is repeated several more times. The scanner goes up just past my waist. Edith has already told me this is a CT of my abdomen so I suspect, with the liver enzymes elevated, this is where she is concentrating.

There is a long wait after the last scan. The nurse emerges from behind the glass.

"The radiologist wants just one more look, Mrs. Deegan? You doing OK out here?"

The dreaded one more look. Is that ever a good thing? I nod and try to smile. She disappears again.

"Take a deep breath and hold," says the voice.

I hold my breath for what seems like a year.

I notice the scanner is moving higher than before, past my stomach and over my chest.

It retreats.

"And you can breathe," says the voice.

Easy for you to say.

I do make an effort to breathe. Can't wait to get out of here and go for a run. There is enough pent up energy in my body to do a marathon right now.

A minute or two goes by. Five. Six. My heart thumps against my chest. It wants to escape and run too. The pounding is all I can hear.

"Mrs. Deegan?"

The radiologist walks toward me. He seems colorless somehow. He looks dour. I want to puke.

"You can sit up now. We're all finished."

Somehow I doubt that.

I swing my legs around and face my accuser.

"Dr. Perez is out of town, but you are an intelligent woman and I don't see any reason to keep this from you."

I feel dizzy, not intelligent. The whole world slows down.

"I'm afraid we have found a small spot on your lower left lung and it appears to be cancer."

My lung? What kind of a sick joke is this? How can it be in my lung? Obviously you don't know that I'm a marathoner. I have the best lungs Shelley has heard all day. That's what she always says. My lungs are awesome.

"I'm sorry Mrs. Deegan. Would you like for me to get your husband for you?"

I manage by best Donna Deegan news anchor smile.

"No, thank you very much, I'm fine," I say, with as much warmth as I can manage.

I slide off the scanner and head for the exit as fast as my feet will take me.

Tim's eyes catch mine the moment I open the door and he's up.

Can't look at him for long. I grab his hand and we hit the hallway.

"Just get me out of here fast," I plead.

He makes a bee line for the door.

"What is it, Donna?"

"Get me to the car Tim, please."

The pictures on the walls speed by. I can't process this. How can this be happening?

We get to the car and I close out the world.

I'm not crying. Just suspended. Like the child who has just received a vaccination in those few moments of shock before it occurs to her to scream.

"It's in my lung, Tim. It's small, but it's there. Of all places, can you believe my lung?"

Tim leans his head back on the seat and closes his eyes.

He squeezes my hand and we sit in silence for a moment. Struggling. He takes a deep breath then turns to face me.

"Edith will have a plan, Donna. You said it's small. She always catches things early. Let's just concentrate on that for now."

All I am thinking is metastatic stage four breast cancer.

"You are going to have to help me live," I say. Even as the words leave my mouth it's as if someone else is saying them. "I cannot let this disease control whatever life I have left."

This triggers thoughts of my children. My son is 12. Drew will be a teenager in a couple of months. His voice is just beginning to change and he's starting to like girls. He's getting thick fuzz above his upper lip and growing so fast that his knees hurt. Drew has given up his glasses now in favor of contacts, but his big chocolate brown eyes blinking at me from behind wire-framed lenses are all I see.

"How wide is the sea, mama?" His question for me when he was six years old.

My daughter Danielle turned 15 in September and is in her first year at Bishop Kenny High School, my alma mater. She is playing volleyball. Her dream. I see her on the court for the first time. She looks up at me, her long dark spiral curls springing. She smiles. Just for me. Pure joy. I shouldn't go here, but I can't help it. They are just beginning to really need me. There is so much of life ahead. With me? Without me?

The flood gates open and I can't close them.

4 | *Kid* Stuff

Fortunately this insanity started while my children were at their father's house. It's given me time to get my bearings. He knows what's happening of course, but agrees I should tell them. I'm not sure at the moment if this is a gift or a curse. Edith has always encouraged me to share only the essentials and tell them I'll be fine. They are older now, though, and certainly the situation is more serious. Is it responsible to tell them not to worry? Will I be fine? For the record, Edith still believes this. A follow up PET scan has confirmed a single isolated lesion. The rest of my body is completely clear.

Sitting in Dan's driveway waiting for the kids to emerge. I'm running through what I'll say about all of this on the ride back to our house.

Danielle is out first, lugging her big purple duffle bag and her back pack. My Amazon girl. How in the world did I ever produce a child with the potential for legs that long? Drew is right behind, his dark thick hair shooting in every direction. Drew isn't a big fan of combs. He's as disorganized as his mother. Three bags, plus cleats are hanging off his shoulders. Balled up clothes threaten to fall through his overstuffed arms.

"Mom can I have a friend over?"

It is the first thing out of Drew's mouth before he even says hello.

Backing the car out of the driveway I'm tempted to say yes and just put off the whole discussion. Because I live such a public life the news will leak out soon if I don't break it myself. The last thing I want is for my kids to hear this from someone else. Still, I'm not planning a three hour speech.

"We'll see buddy. Listen I need to share something with you guys."

Danielle immediately stops fiddling with the radio and turns her large almond shaped eyes my way. Drew edges forward in the back seat and leans his head into the space between the bucket seats.

I am driving now and doing my best to be nonchalant.

"You guys remember I had my tests at Mayo this past week."

Silence.

"Well, it looks like they have found a little spot in my lung that is very likely cancer."

"You have lung cancer?"

Drew says lung like it is a four letter word of the forbidden variety.

"Actually, they think it is my breast cancer, but that it just came back in my lung."

"How do you get breast cancer in your lung?"

"That's what happens sometimes with cancer, Drew. It can start in one place and then show up some place else, but they think it's still the same cancer."

Danielle says nothing.

Drew talks for her.

"So what does that mean?"

The 64-thousand dollar question.

"We don't really know yet, Drew. There is even a very slight possibility it is something else. But we won't know until they take it out. I'll have surgery next week. The good news is Edith says it's small and isolated and that we can remove it. She thinks she can get me right back into remission."

"So you are going to be OK, then."

Drew is a bottom line guy like his mother. Just cut to the chase. Tell me you are going to fix it and let's move on. That is not to say he is shallow. He has a wall around his heart that he will rarely climb.

"I believe I will be, yes. Edith says it is extremely rare to have a recurrence this isolated. She says in all the years she has been practicing, she has only had three cases like this, and all have done very well."

Danielle is still not talking.

"No comment, Danielle?"

"Are you going to lose your hair again?"

"Maybe not. There are new drugs now and Edith says the one she is considering shouldn't make my hair fall out."

The hair thing was always traumatic for Danielle. Drew thought it was pretty cool having a bald mom. He even told me I was beautiful without hair once.

"Cool," Danielle says.

But her full lips are pursed in a way that reminds me of my mother's when she's working over a puzzle. Danielle is a worrier. Another of my traits I wish I hadn't passed on so successfully. The difference between us is that if I'm thinking something it almost always comes out of my mouth.

Danielle will keep it all in. She is more deliberate in her words and more careful of their impact on others.

"So can I have a friend over?" Drew asks again.

He never gives up once he starts.

"Sure, why not."

Hours later, I walk into Danielle's room to find her sitting in her big brown papasan, her favorite reading chair. She immediately takes the book in her lap and covers her face.

"What's up Yellie?"

"Nothing."

Her voice is quivering.

"Talk to me Danielle."

She moves the book to reveal tears streaming down her face.

"I don't want you to have cancer mom," she cries. Her words so soft I can barely hear them, land hard in my chest.

Sitting down on the bed next to her chair, I take her hand. The tiny baby doll fingers I held in her youth are now much longer and more slender than mine.

Now we are both crying.

"I don't want to have it either Danielle. But honey, I am going to do everything I can to be well again. Sometimes we don't understand why things happen, but we just have to trust God and try to find a positive in them."

She nods, sweeping a hand across one of her eyes.

Even as I say the words they sound so inadequate. Do I really believe them? I feel the anger building inside of me. My children should not have to deal with this again. Three times. I wonder if they even remember me before cancer. Will this be what they remember? I put a cap on the rising steam and try to find the words that will comfort yet not mislead my daughter.

"Edith is the best doctor there is, Danielle and she believes I will be OK. She has always been able to catch these spots early so I trust her. I wish I could promise you something here, sweetie, but I can't. All I can tell you is I am going to fight this with everything I have and the medicines are getting better every day. I believe I will beat this."

"OK."

Danielle smiles that heart melting smile I often wish I could wrap in a blanket and carry with me all day. Nothing could be wrong in my world in the presence of that smile.

We hug, and after a few more minutes on the topic we fall into small talk. The subject turns to school and teachers, and volleyball and boys. Just as it should be for a 15-year-old and her mother.

My own mother is already here. She is scheduled for back surgery next month, and will be staying at our home. We'll both be invalids at the same time. She has taken to saying the Rosary non-stop in reaction to all of this. That and telling me that they are going to find out that this is only a boil in my lung and nothing more. She weeps every time she says it though, so I can tell she doesn't really believe this. She's trying. Like the rest of us, she is afraid.

Time to begin the process of telling the rest of my family, my friends, my board members and of course my on air family.

I make a brief announcement on the air, and then on-line through the First Coast News website.

Hi Everyone,

I want to share with you what's been going on with me for the past few days. As most of you know in 1999 I began a battle with breast cancer. It resurfaced in 2002 and as of Wednesday I was expecting to hit a milestone: Five years cancer free.

Well, as usual, Murphy has a twisted sense of humor. During my six month check up I had a couple of numbers that came back just funky enough that my doctor wanted to do a CT scan to make sure nothing was up. It was strange because she usually will see a slight spike here and there and ask me to wait a month for a redo and things are usually fine. This time she just had a gut feeling we needed to check.

The CT scan showed a single small "suspicious" lesion in my lower left lung. A PET scan confirmed the lesion is there, but nothing more anywhere in my body. They are not certain this is cancer. It could be an infected spot in my lung, but those are admittedly long odds. I have no lymph node involvement and Edith says if this is cancer it is what she calls an "isolated metastasis". Again, we won't know this for sure until they can look at the cells under a microscope.

I am having surgery Friday morning to remove the lesion. The thoracic surgeon tells me it is amazing to find such a small single lesion in the lung. Usually if a cancer is found there is it far more complicated and extensive. He feels confident he can remove the lesion with clear borders. If it is cancer I will once again have to undergo chemotherapy. This is of course a drag but there are new drugs out there that are amazing. Edith is confident she can once again put me into full remission if this is the case. The surgeon agrees. (It is even possible I may be able to use drugs that won't make my hair fall out. There is no way to know until we see what's there.)

The wild thing is, the numbers that had concerned Edith have now returned to normal. If that had been the case last week, she would have never ordered these tests and we would have never found this small spot.

Sometimes you have to be grateful for the graces you receive, even if they aren't exactly what you had in mind.

How does the song go? "You can't always get what you want, but if you try sometimes you might find you get what you need."

I feel so fortunate to have a doctor who looks after every small detail. In 2000 I had a headache from taking an antibiotic and she insisted on doing a brain MRI. They found and repaired a large aneurysm that would have almost certainly killed me had it gone undetected. We smiled about that yesterday after we took a huge breath at the results of the PET scan. I truly think I have a guardian angel in Edith.

The National Marathon to Fight Breast Cancer is still full steam ahead. As you know the main goal of the marathon is to find a cure for breast cancer. Fortunately for me, if I must face this I know that at least one of the drugs I will be receiving is right off the bench top and in clinical trials. It has shown amazing promise so far. This is why this fight is so important, not only for me but for hundreds of thousands of women with breast cancer. We are getting there. If you thought I was obnoxious before, well look out.

You all have been my family for a long time.

Thanks for sticking with me through the journey.

Donna

The marathon. I had barely gone five minutes without thinking of it since the idea first popped into my head in 2006. Running guru, Jeff Galloway had been working with me for a year.

Jeff's nature is easy. The pace of his life is not. His commitment to helping people complete a marathon, something very few could do on their own, takes him all over the world. He has training groups in almost every state and some in Europe. Jeff sought me out at a race expo in Jacksonville because he liked that I had combined running with raising money for a cause.

I was working at a booth for my charity, watching this long line of people talking to Jeff at his booth across the aisle. He was so engaged. Casual in running clothes, and a cap, he spent hours on his feet taking questions and hearing praise for his programs. The one statement I must have heard a hundred times was "you've changed my life."

During one of his very few breaks, Jeff walked over to where I was standing selling t-shirts.

"Why don't we train some runners in Jacksonville to do a marathon and ask them to raise pledges for your charity?" he asked.

The marathon is a favorite distance for me so I agreed immediately. Jeff already had a training group in the area. We would simply get our group ready to run the local Jacksonville Marathon.

"If it's a success we'll see about taking it to the next level," Jeff said.

Neither of us had a clear idea of what that next level would be but our partnership was born.

"What's successful to you?" I asked.

"Ten people," he said.

The first year we had 86. We knew we had something. We wanted to focus more on the national stage but beyond getting Jeff's training groups around the country involved, we weren't sure how to do it.

The epiphany came on my birthday. I was having coffee with Edith at Starbucks. We were sitting on two plush purple chairs, saving the world as usual. Between sips of her Cappuccino, she was bemoaning the fact that there was a dwindling supply of money for research, and I was working over ways to raise more money for my charitable foundation. My thoughts were focused on how to get additional runners involved in the Galloway training. Then as if it were the most natural thought in the world, I put down my tall red-eye and heard these words come out of my mouth.

"What if the Donna Foundation partners with Mayo Clinic and we start our own marathon? Mayo would give us a national, even international connection. You'd have your research money and I'd be able to provide more for our underserved women."

Edith's eyes, always bright, could have lit a city block.

"Donna, this is fantastic! Let's do it!"

Her reaction was so swift and forceful I thought it might knock me off the chair.

"This is a done deal, girl. We're going to make this happen," she said.

When the Puerto Rican wonder sets her mind to something, don't bet against her. I'm not keen on taking no for an answer myself. Physically we are both very small women. One dark, one blonde, but our goals are huge. A successful marathon could drive us a long way down the road to those goals.

The key was in the ignition and I was ready to turn it. Jeff would have to provide the road map.

I called him that evening half expecting him to laugh. Let's be honest. You have here a news anchor and a world class researcher, both of whom happen to love running. But those are hardly the credentials for starting a national marathon.

"Jeff, I've done some homework here. There is no U.S. marathon solely to benefit breast cancer," I said.

He didn't laugh. His first words told me everything I needed to know.

"This is an untapped gold mine for the cause."

So that day we began mining for gold. Gold to end breast cancer and to care for those in need living with the disease.

After months of tough negotiations with Mayo, the bones of our race started to emerge.

The course was set. A beautiful trek from the Mayo Clinic, over the Intracoastal Waterway at the J. Turner Butler Bridge. Once at the beach, runners would stream through the streets right along the coast, the ocean always in sight. Then in a unique twist, we'd actually send them onto our hard packed beaches at low tide for two miles. Our beaches are perfect for running and this would be our signature. Runners would pass through Jacksonville Beach, Neptune Beach and Atlantic Beach with its huge moss draped oaks and then make the turn back to the clinic.

After almost five years cancer free, this is my bridge to the role of philanthropist. Becoming a patient, and for the third time mind you, never was part of the plan.

My diagnosis comes as we are in full sprint to the start of our inaugural race.

5 | Size Matters

Dr. Agnew's office is in a small dank building behind St. Luke's hospital. I'm fidgeting nervously in my chair waiting for the receptionist to call my name. Tim takes my hand in his and gives it a squeeze. His hand is big and coarse and real. It is so warm. The exact opposite of my tiny cold fingers. I close my eyes and imagine my whole body curled up in that big generous palm, and I feel momentarily safe.

"Mrs. Deegan."

A nurse with a pleasant face is waiting at the door to the examining rooms. She has a clipboard in her hand. I make my way toward her with Tim's hand in tow.

"Come on back and we'll put you in a room."

She hands me the clipboard.

"Just fill out the information on the first page and Dr. Agnew will be in to talk with you in just a moment."

Edith had wasted no time in recommending Dr. Agnew for my lung surgery.

"This surgeon just came to us at Mayo. He is a rock star," she assured me. I'm anxious to see this boy wonder.

A quick tap on the door and it swings open. In walks a gray haired man with a beard wearing scrubs that look like they've been balled up in a drawer for years. Not exactly what I was expecting. I'm oddly relieved.

"Edith says you're a rock star," I say before I even introduce myself.

"Does she?" he asks. I like the wrinkles around his eyes when he smiles. He strikes me as someone who smiles a lot.

"Edith says you're new. I was expecting some young kid out of medical school."

"I've been around for years. I'm just new to Mayo. I was expecting you to be bigger."

This is the story of my life. As a news anchor I sit on a chair that is adjusted to make me the same height as everyone else. People are always surprised to see that I'm only 5'1". Dr. Agnew's expression tells me though that this is more than just a fascination.

"Do you have something against short people?"

"No, no," he says stifling a laugh. "It's just that seeing you I am sure we won't be able to fit the instruments between your ribs. You are the size of a child."

I have never been one of those people who minded being small, but now I have the uneasy feeling that I am going to be.

"And that means?"

"That means we will have to cut out a piece of your rib to get to your lung. This is going to make your recovery a little slower."

My hand goes instinctively to my left side.

"Can I keep the rib?" Tim asks, out of the blue.

"I would be happy to let you keep it, but that would be against the rules," he says.

I look at Tim like he's from Mars, which he may be.

"How much slower?" I ask. "How much slower on the recovery?"

I pride myself on always recovering quicker than the doctors think I can. In my previous two breast cancer surgeries I was only out of work for a day. Slice me open, take out the trash, sew me up and send me back to the front lines.

"You won't be able to do much of anything for several weeks. We'll get you up walking immediately after the surgery, but you'll have to take it easy for a while. I don't think you will feel like doing much more though. This is not an easy procedure."

"So how long in the hospital? Two days? Three?"

"You will be there for four or five days. Listen I've heard about you. I know you are active. I will get you out of there just as soon as I can, but this is an invasive surgery. This is your lung. We are cutting through your ribs. It's going to take time to heal."

"I will go crazy if you make me sit in a hospital bed for five days. I am hoping to be back to work in a week."

He smiles and shakes his head.

"Not a chance," he says.

"And my running?"

"A month at least."

That's so ridiculous to me I ignore it.

"And my overall ability to run. How will taking out a piece of my lung affect that?"

"You won't even notice the difference. I should be able to get all the way around the lesion without taking out more than 10 percent of your lung. Besides, I hear you are a blow hard."

Now this is not an insult. It's actually a compliment. In my pre-op lung tests I had to blow into a tube to gauge my lung capacity. More than ten years of marathoning has paid off. I blew 139 percent of what my lungs should be able to handle. This made me an official inductee into the "blow hard hall of fame" or so the nurse told me.

"It's still going to be at least a month before you can run," he says again.

Despite this, I like him. I can tell he doesn't fit the Mayo mold at all. Not that I don't love my Mayo docs. I do. But they are all well schooled in the "Mayo way". They walk in lock step. They follow the rules in the Mayo hand book. Women who work there aren't even allowed to wear open-toed shoes for God's sake. To say they are buttoned down would be unfair to buttons. They aren't just buttoned down. They are buttoned up, and sideways with zippers and pins just to be safe.

Anyone who doesn't iron his scrubs is cool in my book. I think he is comfortable in his skin. And I trust he will be comfortable in mine.

Besides, I'll show him I don't fit the mold either. I'm not your average patient. I'm in full battle mode. Translated, I am frightened out of my mind.

6 | Taking Out the Trash

September 21th, 2007

"Hola Padre!" I look up from my holding cell in pre-op to see the cherubic face of my dear friend Father Greg Fay.

Father Greg and I have known each other since I was in high school. He set the entire Bishop Kenny campus abuzz when he went flying onto the campus in 1978 in his silver anniversary corvette with red leather interior. Are priests allowed even to touch red leather? It was a present from his parents to celebrate his graduation from the seminary. Hello? Anybody heard of that vow of poverty thing?

From the first day it was obvious this was going to be no ordinary priest. And that is exactly why he connected with a bunch of teenagers. He has always been someone with whom I feel comfortable just letting it all hang out. I could tell him anything and everything and I have. It makes confession so much easier when you are talking with an approachable stand-in for The Big Guy.

"I brought you Communion," he says, holding up a metal container.

"I have some good scotch too, if you'd rather." He pats his pocket, raising his eyebrows in invitation.

"I'm going to be out cold in a few minutes so I don't think the scotch could be fully appreciated at the moment," I reply.

"Good enough then, first let me give you absolution."

"But I haven't confessed anything yet."

"Well, that's the beauty of people in your situation. You get a free pass just before surgery."

I am not about to ask just what situation I would have to be in to get this heavenly reprieve. Hey, when a priest offers you a don't ask, don't tell, no penance required get out of jail free card, you take it and run.

I receive the Eucharist and then he crosses my head with Holy Oil and gives me The Anointing of the Sick, which we used to call the Last Rites.

I'm feeling good about the name change.

"Ready to take a nap?" the nurse asks rounding the curtain.

"You're gonna do fine kiddo," Father Greg says and places his hand on mine. "Extra prayers all day. No worries, OK?"

"Hey, you're the one who just gave me the Last Rites," I say.

"Anointing of the Sick," he corrects me. And with a wink he is gone.

"Do you have a Living Will?" The nurse is going down her checklist. Countdown to blastoff.

"No, I don't. I know I should," I answer.

"We all should," Tim says.

True, but he's not the one about to have his rib cut out and his lung punctured.

"You need to sign this," she says, and hands me a pen and a clipboard with some papers.

"What is it? Your basic 'we can kill you if we want and you can't sue us,' thing?"

"You got it," she says.

"You'll need to take your jewelry off too."

"I've taken all of it off except my wedding band and you're not getting that," I say and just that quick my eyes fill with tears.

Damn those things. They always appear right when I'm trying to be most brave. It's such an irritation.

"If your hand swells, we might have to cut the ring off and you don't want that," she insists.

The position of my body for this incursion is almost grotesque. Because they want my ribs spread as much as possible, they will place me on my side and tape my arm over my head in such a way that it will almost dislocate my shoulder.

"Rules are rules," she says.

I turn to my husband.

"I am just about over these rules. First you can't keep my rib. Now I have to give up my ring."

As usual I am doing my best to joke my way out of an uncomfortable situation. Anything to stop the tears.

It's not working.

My heart is pounding and my nose is turning red. Little beads of sweat are starting to play around my mouth. I look at Tim, eyes pleading.

Tell me I'm OK. Tell me you'll make it alright.

His clear blue eyes are locked on me with such intensity that I could dive right into them and swim away.

"Donna, it's OK."

There is something so beautiful about hearing the man you love say your name. I wish he could come with me into this Never-Neverland for a few hours. Then I'd be safe for sure.

"I'll take good care of your ring and it will be back on your finger when you wake up. I'll wear it right here on my pinky. It won't leave my hand."

I nod, twist the ring off my finger and place it on his little finger. He grabs my hand and plants a kiss where my ring should be.

It is almost a relief to start counting backwards into the darkness.

I awake to the muffled sounds of vaguely familiar voices. The light is disorienting at first but then brings things slowly into focus.

I'm still here.

A horrible ache in my shoulder punctuates that point.

Two large tubes are protruding from my left side. Reddish yellow goo is lurching back and forth inside them. My heartbeat is drumming its way across a monitor beside me.

"Hello, my love." Tim's voice wraps me in its embrace. My ring is on my finger.

"Am I OK?" It's tough to get my mouth around the syllables. I've always had a difficult time coming out of anesthesia.

"Everything went beautifully, Donna. Dr. Agnew got all the cancer."

At first I say nothing.

"So we are sure that's what it is then?" I don't even want to say the word.

For a moment, Tim doesn't register what I'm asking. Then the light bulb comes on. There was an outside chance this could be an infection, or something less sinister than cancer. A boil, as my mother suggested.

"Yes," he says, momentarily shifting his eyes to his hands. "Same kind as before. Dr. Agnew was able to get nice clean borders around it though. It's all gone."

I nod. At the moment, I am too tired and too fuzzy to formulate much of a coherent thought. I was expecting this news anyway.

"I do have something really exciting to tell you," Tim says. "Edith came to me just before the surgery and asked for my consent to collect your tumor cells for research. She's going to use them to develop more targeted therapies. She's hoping to do this with a lot of patients but you are the first one."

My left shoulder is screaming so loudly I can barely hear him.

"That's great news, honey," I say, rubbing it.

"Shoulder hurts huh?"

"Really bad."

"Want me to call the nurse and get you something for pain?"

I hate pain medications. They make me sick to my stomach, loopy (OK loopier than normal) and they make the contents of my bowels the annoying equivalent of relatives who come to visit and never leave. Consequently after all of my surgeries I ask for Tylenol as soon as possible.

Dr. Agnew warned me this was going to be different. He was right in spades.

"Call Father Greg," I say. "I'm ready for my scotch."

7 | Please Release Me, Let Me Go

September 24, 2007

It's been four days. I'm sitting in my hospital bed glaring at my doctor. They have mercifully removed the alien appendages from my side. I'd threatened to rip them out, stitches and all if they didn't. Now though the oozing goo is saturating the bandages they placed over the incisions every few minutes sending the sticky bloody mixture trickling down my side. I feel gross. Haven't washed my hair in days and I'm restless beyond words.

Damn, I hate sitting still.

The only activity in my days is my hourly trip down the hall with my IV pole in tow. I have taken to speed walking now just to irritate the nurses. I almost ran into one of them yesterday. This is my idea of entertainment.

"Why can't I leave today? Look at me. I'm practically running down the halls now," I say.

Apparently an x-ray of my lung shows that it still has too much fluid in it and is in danger of collapse.

Yet I'm certain if I don't get out of here soon my mind is in danger of collapse. I am desperate.

"Donna, let's give it one more day and look again," he says. "I know I can't keep someone like you in bed for long. I understand you need to get out of here, and I am doing all I can to get you out. But trust me you do not want your lung to collapse."

True enough. But my lung feels fine as far as I can tell. I did have quite the failed experiment a couple of nights ago. I insisted I didn't need my pain meds anymore and asked the nurses to bring me Tylenol. By the time I realized I wasn't going to make it, my side was on fire. A red hot poker had been plunged into it and I swear someone was twisting it, pulling on it, pushing it. The slightest movement sent me into space.

And there was no turning back the pain once it started. The nurse finally had to dope me up enough to knock me out.

All of this is beside the point. I want out.

"One more day, doc. That's all you're getting from me. I need to move. Do you understand?"

"I do understand, Donna."

And I think he does. This is not his first rodeo after all and neither is it mine. I like Dr. Agnew and I know I'm acting like a petulant child, but there is only so much time I can sit here stuck with my own crazy head. If I am moving I can move past this. I need to get back to my life. Sitting here hour after hour only magnifies my fears.

A steady stream of well wishers and friends are all telling me what a great fighter I am and how I am going to beat this again and blah blah blah. They mean well. I say all the right things back to them but in the quiet of my room after they are gone my good friend fear is waiting for me.

He seems comfortable in my head. And why shouldn't he be? He has been there for so long now he has his own apartment. He started moving his junk in years ago, unpacking worry, and stress, and guilt. When we meet up, I do my best not to look him in the eye.

Much easier to glare at my doctor and demand release.

8 | ✑Told You So

Ten days since my surgery and today I'm going back to work. Dr. Agnew says I should wait another week, but I'm ready. Being cooped up at home with my mother, God love her, has taken its toll. I am no longer even pretending to be a nice person. It's not her fault. I just don't like to be fussed over. She will be having her own surgery soon, and I'll return the favor. She won't like it any better than me.

The lack of sleep isn't helping. Haven't slept through the night since I got home. I'm starting to feel somewhat better but still can't find a comfortable position in bed. A couple of days ago, I wrote about it all in my journal. It was my way of telling those following my progress on the web that I would be back on the anchor desk soon.

*   *   *

```
Hello Everyone!
Wow, what a difference a week makes. I am feeling
downright human again! I will tell you though,
```

with some degree of sadness that I am giving up on my dream of one day becoming a wide receiver for the Jaguars.

Coach had always told me that my size(5'1" & 102 pounds) might be a limiting factor, but I was undaunted until last week's surgery.

Because I am such a dinky person, the doctors had to actually cut out a piece of one of my ribs to get to my lung so they could remove the lesion.

I am here to tell you this is NOT FUN. Now your girl is no sissy. This, as you know, is not my first barbeque.

But this broken rib thing is not something I wish to repeat.

There is no comfortable position. No matter if I sit, stand, stretch out, right side, left side. After ten days I still feel as if someone has taken a hammer to my side.

As I say though, this is a huge improvement over last week when the hammer was a steamroller.

I now have new respect for Ernest Wilford, Matt Jones, and the rest of the Jaguars receiving corps.

Guys I TOTALLY understand now why sometimes it just doesn't seem quite worth it to stretch out for those passes.

My ribs hurt just thinking about it. You may rest

assured anyway that your jobs are safe. It looks
like so much fun to catch those spiraling balls and
streak for the end zone.

But from now on, dreams aside, I'm planning to
keep my ribs intact and in the stands where they
belong. I'll just have to keep my day job. Speaking
of which, I will see you all on Wednesday!

Donna

*   *   *

I have never in my life had any severe pain hang on this long. Even so
I'm trying to wean myself off of the pain meds believing sincerely that if
I'm constipated for another week I am going to have to kill someone.

Dressing gingerly, I realize there is no way a bra is going on this body.
The straps sit right on the incisions in my side and back and that isn't
going to work.

Who cares. It's not like my double A ta-tas are going to come
tumbling out of my jacket. Bandaids will do.

"You've lost too much weight, Donna. You don't even fill out that
jacket anymore," my mother says, as I appear in the kitchen to grab
my keys.

"It's not that, Mom, I just don't have on the Victoria's Secret, water
filled, padded, push-up, if you don't have it flaunt it anyway bra."

I must admit though, looking down at my body, my mother has a
point. My clothes are hanging on me. I haven't been eating much since

my surgery. There is something about pain that seems to trump hunger.

"You're too skinny," she repeats.

This from the 4'10" woman who weighs 85 pounds with all her clothes on plus rocks in her pockets.

Personally, I have always been of the opinion that it's not possible for me to be too skinny. At least this was my attitude until I got into my 40s and all the weight seemed to come off my face and boobs first. Never my thighs. God forbid! A skinny face shows more wrinkles. Not good in my business.

My mother looks up at me, red hair framing her green-gray eyes.

"You need to start eating."

"Thank you, Mother, I'll do that."

Conversation Over.

The truth is, it isn't just the pain that's keeping me from eating. During my time at home I've started reading everything I can about foods that are good for cancer patients and those that are not, and as far as I can tell, nothing I've ever eaten in my life is good for me. Meat is poison. Sugar feeds cancer. Don't even get me started on milk. I should be taking 47 different supplements. Coffee is bad. Coffee is good. I need to alkalize my system. I'm too acidic! I am afraid to put anything in my mouth.

Edith thinks all of this is utter foolishness. I often give her grief because she survives on a diet of oatmeal and crackers. "Gray food" her friend Joni calls it. She hydrates with Diet Coke.

Edith is sure that what I eat or don't, won't impact my cancer in any way.

"You simply couldn't consume enough of anything to make a

significant difference. Life is too short for you to waste your time on this, Donna," she tells me.

I'm not convinced. But I'm not educated either. At the moment I am paralyzed by what I do not know. Reading way too much in that vast dumping ground that is the internet. My brain is in overload with conflicting information. I know I need to find a more reliable source.

As a news anchor, I've become increasingly concerned that people seem to give bloggers as much credit as they do trained journalists who have a set of principals and checks and balances. Bloggers can say whatever they want. I have to have two sources and both sides before I can say anything. Therefore, while I may read a blog, I don't give it nearly the credibility I give to a reporter who I know is at least trying to get to the truth.

Edith is much the same way with research. If something hasn't been studied for years with a sufficient test group, and there isn't a control, she is simply not going to give it credibility. I get it. She is a scientist. A very good one. Then again, Edith has never had cancer. She can't possibly know how desperate it feels to have zero control over your own body. She can wait 20 years for something to pan out. I don't feel like I have that luxury. It doesn't mean I'm going to go off chasing rainbows. It does mean I am going to keep my mind open.

More and more I am considering seeing a holistic or integrative medicine doctor for some sound advice on things I can do to make my body healthier.

I have an ally in Dr. Agnew. During my follow-up examination in his office, I asked him his opinion of holistic medicine.

"I just feel like I owe it to Tim, to my children and to myself to explore every possible way to stay alive," I explained. "I've had this three times now. Why? Maybe it's something I'm doing or not doing. Eating or not eating. At the very least I want to try to control those things I can control."

"I have had a holistic doctor diagnose yellow fever when I was unable to," he said. "It's like anything else, Donna. There are very good holistic doctors and there are quacks. You just have to choose wisely. But absolutely I think this is something you should explore. You will have to do more than change your diet though."

My 'not in the Mayo mold' doc gave me the thumbs up I was looking for.

Edith will not be open to anything of this nature until I finish my chemotherapy. At the moment I haven't even started. Have to heal for a few weeks before Edith will decide which drugs to give me. Let my body recover so that I can take drugs that will tear it down. If I start the chemo too soon, my wounds would stay just that. Then, by knocking down my immune system, the drugs can fight the cancer. It all seems so counterintuitive.

I do trust Edith when it comes to the best medicines to use. After all, I was first diagnosed eight years ago and I am still here. The drugs have done their job. And they are getting easier to tolerate. But she doesn't have all the answers. No one does.

"When you do, I'll close the books on everything else," I tell her. "Until then, I'm searching just like you."

For now, I'm content to search for my keys. They are nowhere in sight. I haven't driven in almost a month. I search everywhere. My purse, my make-up bag, my dresser, the bathroom. Finally I open the drawer where Tim, the organized one, keeps his keys and there they are. He had placed them there for safe keeping.

"I'll see you at dinner time, Mom."

"OK, Sweetie." She reaches to hug me.

"Not too hard," I say, giving her a light squeeze. "Can you get the door for me?"

Even the front door is too much weight for me to pull.

By the time I am through my first newscast I am in horrible pain. In order for me to project my voice from the news desk, my diaphragm gets quite the work out. I hadn't even remotely considered this when I decided to return to work.

After the 11p.m. broadcast I'm in as much pain as when I first came out of surgery. Tim wants me to cry uncle.

"Just tell them you can't do it yet, Donna. Go ahead and take the rest of the week off and you can go back on Monday."

"No way. What kind of message does that send? I can't show up, say I'm fine and then disappear for the rest of the week."

I double my pain meds and steal a sleeping pill from my mother.

"Besides," I say, "I am not going to give Dr. Agnew the satisfaction of saying I told you so."

9 | *Everyone Sweats*

October 31, 2007

It is Halloween and I'm going through mounds of e-mails that I've mostly neglected since my surgery. The date is significant. It is five years to the day of my last chemotherapy treatment and I am stepping back into that world I'd hoped I left behind. Starting to get nauseated just thinking about more chemo, but at least for the moment, I only have to take pills. No needles. This is huge for both me and the poor souls who have to stick "the veinless one."

After much debate Edith has settled on a drug called Xeloda. From what she says, the side effects are few. The most significant is that it will very likely make my hands and feet swell, turn red and peel. Not the best news for a marathoner, but hey, I'll take peeling over puking any day.

And as an added bonus, my hair won't fall out. When I first got on this merry-go-round almost a decade ago, I thought the whole bald thing would be no big deal. I figured I'd just pop on a wig. Not worry about doing my hair for the news every day. No fuss, no muss. It turned out to be one of the most traumatic parts of the treatment for me. A visible sign to all that virtually screamed "sick girl here!" with a big neon arrow pointing at my shiny head. Every time I looked in the mirror I saw the girl with cancer and it became who I was. I could see it reflected in the eyes of people who looked at me. Pity.

Damn, I must be bad off.

The fact that I will not be facing those pitying looks, not staring back at the sick girl in the mirror, is a relief. One less wall between me and the finish line.

Edith is still debating giving me a second drug that would alter the state of my blood vessels to make delivery of the first drug more effective. It isn't likely to make my hair fall out either. That is not the biggest concern however. Edith is uneasy about this drug. It has a rather high mortality rate and tends to thin the blood. At one time I had an aneurysm, a weakness in a vein in my head that was surgically repaired. She wants to make sure the drug won't be a threat to that vein. All in all, I'm just thankful there are options and that Edith is the one choosing them.

For as much grief as I give her, and I do, there isn't a day that goes by that I am not grateful she is my doctor and my friend. She is so real, so down to earth, that sometimes it's easy to forget her brilliant mind.

She is widely regarded as one of the best in the world.

Edith is responsible for what is arguably one of the most significant breakthroughs in breast cancer research in 30 years.

She developed a clinical trial which combined a drug called Herceptin with chemotherapy. The result was a more than 50 percent decrease in the rate of recurrence for a particularly vicious type of breast cancer. The combination was a huge success even for those with advanced disease.

Another of my running pals, Kristie Naines is still here today because of that breakthrough. Almost four years ago the diminutive blonde, even smaller than me, was diagnosed with Her-2 positive breast cancer. It was well into her lymph system.

"I had a number of doctors tell me there was nothing they could do for me," she said. "Basically, go travel, have a nice life, but prepare yourself for the inevitable. I had a three year old child and this answer just wasn't going to cut it for me. Then I met Edith and she gave me hope. Her answer was the exact opposite. I'll never forget hearing the words come out of her mouth. 'You've been cancer free since your surgery and we're going to keep you that way.' And she has." Kristie told me.

Edith points to women like Kristie when people lament that the years of research have yet to find a magic bullet for breast cancer.

"People want to know why we haven't found a cure. I tell them that we are curing women every day," she told me.

Her focus now, and one of the ways in which she plans to use the money from our first marathon, is to tailor treatments to individual patients.

As I speak, the cancerous cells that were removed from my lungs are under her careful study. That's the future of breast cancer treatment in Edith's mind. At least the immediate future. You and I may have the same type of cancer, but it may do something entirely different in my body than it does in yours. The future will treat us like people instead of numbers. On a personal level, Edith has always done this.

As a treatment option, it hasn't been so easy.

I feel good that the research dollars from the race will be in her capable hands.

In the meantime I'll continue with my own research. I'm gathering more information for the holistic path I plan to take after the chemo is done.

An email on the subject from Loretta Haycook is among some two hundred in my inbox this morning. She is a member of my running team, and a veteran of more than 40 marathons. I have no idea why I asked her for advice on this topic beyond the fact that everything about her says that her mind, body and spirit are humming along in harmony like few I've ever met. At every run, Loretta appears to be as excited as she was on the first day I met her.

Donna,

Here is the doctor I would like you to contact. A few years ago a husband of one of my running friends was extremely ill with pancreatitis. He had traveled all over trying to get the best care; finally he found this physician here at the beach.

Dr. Bridget Freeman is a trained oncologist, but I don't know if she even practices that. She is a holistic physician. My friend's husband is cured! He now is back to running a 5 min mile and doing great. He and his wife attribute his good health to the holistic approach.

I don't know everything about her. She does not at all discourage current treatments for illness; she does think she can help w/ overall wellness by the holistic approach.

My friend is Linda White. Her husband, Johnny White is the one who was so sick. You and Tim may already know them. I emailed her and asked for the name of his physician, but I did not tell her it was you. She offered her help if you want to talk and see if you even want to contact Dr. Freeman. Linda goes to UNF (The University of North Florida) and speaks to the health classes about his recovery. I hope this helps. I am a believer after seeing Johnny before and after her care.

Take care, Loretta

I do know Linda. Not well, but Tim does. She and Johnny are his friends from back in the day when triathlons were his weekly routine. I print off Loretta's email and set it beside my computer.

This is for after chemo. Right now I have a race to organize. Thank God for the diversion!

I pop my three large pink pills with a shudder (I am not a good pill taker) and dive back into my emails.

The next one is from my former news director Mike McCormick.

From: Mike McCormick

To: Donna Deegan

remember life is a marathon . . .

you will hit some walls on the way to the finish . . .

but you know how to power through . . .

as you well know, finishing is the real victory . . .

and how you finish is more important than where . . . .

you've got the class, the strength and the stamina

to run the whole race . . . .

mmc

Through Rose Colored Glasses

I hope you're right Mike.

I skip past the rest that don't look marathon related. There is so much to do to get ready for our inaugural and there are literally dozens of emails concerning the race.

How many race brochures should we print? What color should we make the t-shirts for the medical team? Have the measurements for the course been sent to USA Track and Field for certification?

Most of the messages are from Theresa Price. Theresa is the mastermind of Jacksonville's Office of Special Events and has been taking all of my grand ideas and putting them into motion. I'm in awe of her ability to get things done. My head would literally explode if I tried to do as many things at once as Theresa is able to manage.

She will be at the control center of the race when I abandon all my responsibilities on the day of the marathon and hit the road with thousands of my closest friends.

It's selfish of me, but after all, the race is called 26.2 With Donna. I really have to run.

My mind wanders to race day. Three and a half months to go. I'm only just starting to run again.

Can I do it? Maybe I can get myself up to half marathon distance by then. What if my feet are so swollen I can't run? But I have to! People are counting on me.

The more I think, the more frantic my thoughts become. My feet are starting to ache already and I just took my first pills.

The phone rings, bringing me back to the present. It's Theresa.

"Hey you," I say, ready to plunge back into the details of the race.

"Hey, just wondering what you want to do about the certification?"

We launch into a tedious discussion of what we need to get to the Boston Athletic Association in order to be listed as a Boston Qualifier.

Boston is Mecca for any serious marathon runner. It is the only marathon for which runners must post a qualifying time to gain entry. We have received dozens of emails about this and we still haven't received the paperwork that would do the trick.

We go over the other issues on Theresa's list and hang up.

So much to do, but it's joyful work. Two years in the planning and we are finally almost to the starting line.

This race has become like one of my children. Its success is personal. Not just because I have had breast cancer three times, though clearly that is a motivator, but because of the bonds I've now built with so many.

Stories of survival and loss are pouring into the 'Why I'm Running' section of the breastcancermarathon.com website but I don't need to look farther than our own training family to find them.

The next message in my inbox is from one of our Galloway training directors Amanda Napolitano. Our group has just completed its 16 mile training run: A scenic tour through Fort Clinch State Park in Fernandina Beach. Each week we try to mix it up, run in a different location. This keeps it interesting but also makes it fairer to our members who live in every different zip code of the First Coast. Since my surgery I've been unable to make the training runs, so Amanda sends me weekly progress reports. This one includes some sad news.

"A member of our running group recently lost a family member to breast cancer," she writes. "My prayer list continues to grow. I knew you would want to know."

Underneath is a forward from one of our marathoners.

Amanda,

I am sorry I have missed the runs the last few weeks. I am hoping to get caught up again. My sister in law has been in and out of the hospital the past month. Well on Sunday 10/21/07 she lost her fight with breast cancer and passed away after a battle for 2.5 years. This gives me even more purpose to run as she was an inspiration and one of the people I was hoping would be cured. I am not sure when I will rejoin the group, but will again pick up my training for the full marathon this week. I am praying for the group and hope that all your runs are well. I will meet with you all again. I miss you all.

Danielle Stenli

More fuel for the legs. We all have our reasons for running. There are many with connections to breast cancer like Danielle's. But all of us with challenges, and that would be, well, all of us are finding out just how much we are connected.

Take Ike Brown. He has no connection to breast cancer but he is a survivor.

Ike is a Jacksonville police officer and I am fairly certain, an angel on earth. Whenever there is a hostage situation, or someone needs to be talked down from the ledge, somehow Ike just happens to be right there. Somehow he is able to talk people into doing the most extraordinary things.

He loves the criminals just like he loves the victims. This is what makes Ike special. People are people to him. All in pain and all within his healing reach.

He could choose to see things much differently and no one would blame him. Ike lost his son in a horrible shooting accident the year before. The unintended victim of a bullet that was meant for someone else.

He could have chosen revenge. But do you know what he did instead? He went to the jail where the young man who shot his boy was locked up. He told him to change his life. That he would help. He told him he forgave him and that he would do all he could to help him turn his life around and that is exactly what he proceeded to do. Instead of treating this young man like a lost cause, he treated him just like his lost son. That is my definition of an angel.

Ike runs with us because he needs communion. He gives us strength and we give it back to him. Everyone sweats.

10 | Medal of Honor

November 15, 2007

"It's perfect, Kurtis. Absolutely perfect."

A prototype of our inaugural race medal is dangling from a ribbon in my hand. It's yet another beautiful creation by my buddy, fellow runner, and artist Kurtis Loftus.

Kurtis runs with Tim's group on Saturdays. Every group has a name. Theirs is "The Fasties." This is the crew that is always up for a Boston qualifier.

We have groups of every pace. From those who like to set weekly land speed records to those who are happy to be out walking the distance. Our walkers call themselves "The Lovers." Their group leader, John TenBroeck, known to most simply as "Dr. John" likes to tell people the reason for the name. "We are out here so long that we have to love it!"

Kurtis and I have been over and over the elements of the race medal. It has to be unique. For some runners getting the medal is just a sidebar to crossing the finish line. But for many, it's the prize. The bling's the thing. Some even choose the races they want to run based on what medal they like best.

Standing in the front room of this old Jacksonville Beach home that

Kurtis has converted to an office, I hold it up to the light and the effect is stunning. It's a sun catcher. Our trademark pink "running ribbon" is in the center in a look that resembles stained glass. It is surrounded by a turquoise background with a dark blue wave rolling through the middle.

"The running ribbon had to be the centerpiece," he says. "Everyone loves it."

The running ribbon has been a huge hit. Still remember the day I chose it. Or rather it chose me. I was sitting at a long table in meeting room at the Dalton Agency. Michael Munz, who is the Executive Vice President at the ad agency, had directed his team to come up with concepts for our race logo. There were four.

The first had the name of the race with a sort of a mod looking pink running woman. I nixed that one almost immediately because I didn't want to give anyone the impression we were a race just for women.

The second used the pink breast cancer ribbon as the "O" in Donna. It was clean. Simple. Liked it. Didn't love it.

The third was a design that somewhat mimicked the look of the logo for The Donna Foundation. A pink ribbon separated the "with" and the "Donna". The words "The National Marathon to Fight Breast Cancer" arched like a rainbow over the top.

Then there was the running ribbon. A pink, sneaker wearing ribbon, with arms. I thought it was unique but something about it bugged me.

I stared at all four and started to point out the attributes I liked in each.

Then Michael simply shook his head.

"There is no choice here," he said.

He pushed the running ribbon out from the group.

"This is your logo."

"I'm not sure," I said.

"I am," he shot back with a smirk. "This will catch on with people. It is totally unique. Forget the regular pink ribbon. You are creating your own. It says with one picture what you are all about. You don't even need the words. Runners will see this and immediately identify with the cause. It's perfect."

But it wasn't perfect.

For a moment we sort of sat and glared at each other. Michael and I are both always right, you understand. This makes our friendship interesting to say the least. We first met each other years ago through our mutual addiction to politics. Sometimes we agreed. Sometimes we didn't. But no matter how spirited the debate, neither one of us was ever wrong.

As I was about to explain that this was not his decision on the logo, but mine, I realized what was causing my hesitation.

"It doesn't look like it's running," I said. "That's what bugs me. Can we pick up the pace a little bit with this guy? Maybe lift his knee a bit and get those arms swinging?"

Michael made the adjustments and our logo was born.

Now, I can hardly believe I'm holding in my hand our first race medal. Soon my running ribbon will be hanging around the necks of thousands of runners from across the country and the world. The thought sends a tingle down my spine. I can see them all in my mind, crossing the finish line, arms raised, exhausted but satisfied in their accomplishment. Teary eyed as volunteers offer each a medal. Hugging their loved ones. It's as clear to me as if it were happening right now.

"And Kurtis, you got my dolphins in there!"

Cast in silver on each side, the dolphins frame the name of the race at the top of the medal.

"I know how much you wanted them and they were a perfect signature for the beach. I thought showing them jumping on either side was also a symbol for hope."

Hope, of course. Susan would like that. The dolphins were for her.

In one of our last conversations before she died, she told me to look for the dolphins. They were here favorite creature. "Whenever you see the dolphins, jumping and playing, you'll know that's me," she said.

Dolphins are considered good luck. When I see them I always give a little wave and say, "Hello, Susan!"

My heart aches at the thought of her. If she were here she would tell me to cut it out.

"I'm fine, Donna," I can hear her say.

Susan told me she reached that revelation one day while walking on the beach.

"A calm just came over me and I realized that whether I'm here or someplace else, I'm good. Breast cancer can't take that from me," she said.

Now she is in that someplace else and I find myself wondering if she is indeed good. I want to believe she is. I miss her so much. Susan would love this medal. I'm sure of that.

"It's wonderful Kurtis. Don't change anything," I say.

"Can I get that in writing? I think that's a first."

"Come on, am I that bad?"

"Do you want me to answer that?"

"Not really. Thank you for putting up with me."

I give Kurtis a quick hug and walk out of his yellow cottage into a cloudless November day.

11 | *C*ity of Angels

December 26, 2007

Stepping off the plane, the heat hits me like a wave.

My hands and feet, now fully peeled at least two times over from the effects of the chemo are swollen and throbbing, but I don't care.

My cell phone is off, my computer is in Jacksonville, and I am with the people I care about most in the world. I have often been accused of failing to disconnect, but when I am here in Costa Rica that is never a problem. At the moment I relish the thought.

Amanda is handling my race email. Theresa and her staff are running circles around everyone, working their magic to get the final road closures, the tents, the bleachers, the aid stations all ready for race day. The TV station can't even reach me.

I am mercifully free. All thoughts of everything beyond my family and my little piece of paradise are banished for the week. It is not even an effort to keep it this way. This will likely be our last trip to Costa Rica with the kids for a while. Both have announced they are officially "over" spending their entire Christmas break away from their friends.

Danielle is a bit nostalgic about it all. Drew is already asking what time our flight leaves for home. Tim is completely buzzed on the knowledge that in about two hours, the time it takes to rent our car and get to the beach, he will be surfing the warm fast waves of Playa Grande. I am just happy to soak it all in. I have five books, all of them mindless, and I am already dreaming about which hammock I will be lounging in to read them.

We will spend our first four days at the beach, then pack up and head for the rain forest and the Arenal volcano.

"I can't wait to see everyone," says Danielle as we lug our backpacks into the rental car.

"I can't wait to live up north so I never have to be this hot again," Drew says. He hardly knows what to do with his hands without his cell phone.

The roads are surprisingly well maintained as we make our way from Liberia southwest through the towns that will take us to our destination.

"Your Dad would never believe this," I say to Tim.

"Nope."

We smile at the thought of our big family trip here two years before.

Christmas of 2005 we loaded up most of the Deegan clan and brought everyone here for a family vacation. Chevy Chase had nothing on us. Twenty-six of us from grandparents all the way to toddlers made this very trek. The moment we hit the road, however, it was clear the driving, at least, would be a mess. Costa Rica is known for horrible road conditions, but this was something beyond anything Tim and I had ever experienced.

There were potholes every few feet the size of small cars. Almost none of the roads had been paved, and we had to drive at a crawl just to ensure that we wouldn't fall into one of them. The speed wasn't really a problem though because one of our rental vans was apparently ailing. It had absolutely no pick- up and if we were lucky on the down hills we could grab enough momentum to get up to about 20 miles per hour, just in time to brake for another pothole. You had to avoid the big ones, but the smaller ones were everywhere. Every few moments we would drop 'THUNK' into another divot. A trip that would usually take us a little more than an hour took nearly three. Add to that the fact that Tim's mom, Margie had a horrible spell with a disc in her back and, well, you get the picture. It was a miserable drive from the airport.

Once at the hotel we had a blast surfing, playing, and just hanging out together. The kids danced to the song 'Gasolina'. The adults drank their weight in Imperial. We went zip lining and hiking at a nearby volcano called Rincon De La Viejo, covered ourselves in volcanic mud, and swam in the hot springs nearby.

On the way back to the airport, our good friend Louis, who owns the hotel where we stay, told us he had a great "shortcut" that would get us there more quickly.

"And the roads will be much better," he said.

A few miles into the trip it was evident this would be no shortcut. The potholes were not the size of small cars they were the size of small busses. We became hopelessly lost. The van had finally gotten so bad that at the bottom of each hill, my brother-in-law Terry had to order everyone out to push. The kids were scared. Tim's sister, Mary Pat was sitting next to me in our car, her knuckles were white as she clung to the handle on the door.

The only person who wasn't completely freaked out was Margie. Tim's mom has an adventurous spirit to start with. We had been able to procure some good pain medication for her back and she was positively delighted during the drive.

After finally deciding to cross a patch of water the depth of which was unknown, we passed an overturned, burned out car that looked like it might have at one time been a Hummer.

At this point we were fairly sure we were all going to die. Then, just like that we popped out onto the highway. Safe at last!

"Tell Louis, thanks for the shortcut," Tim's father Paul said, shaking his head as we finally recognized at least a version of civilization.

Now of course we pull out our pictures and the whole ordeal, burned out car and all, is part of the lore, our fantastic journey. Then, not so much.

Streaking down the smooth dark pavement today seems almost surreal in comparison.

"These roads are as good as the ones at home," I say.

"I know, Dad would never believe it."

"Don't forget to stop at the super mercado, Timatao."

"Of course, Mi Amore."

A few miles from the hotel we load up on all the sundries we will need for the week. Toothpaste, shampoo, sun block. I grab a few apples, some cheese and crackers and we're off.

We pass Kike's the little bar and restaurant where we always hold our "international pool competitions", El Horno De Leña, our favorite pizza joint, the turtle museum, and then into the friendly confines of Los Tortugas.

"Hola, Jefe!"

Alexi, the groundskeeper greets us, arms wide open, a grin as big as a Cadillac. His maple eyes glow almost to the point of looking moist. The word 'jefe' means chief or boss in Spanish. Alexi first used the phrase with us when Paul and the family were here. Paul, being the head of the clan was always greeted as 'jefe'.

Now when it's just us, Tim gets the title. I love to take Alexi to task on this. "Alexi, no," I point to myself. "Jefe".

He laughs in a high pitched tone and shakes his head.

"No, no, no," he says.

In all the years we've been coming here, I have never seen Alexi seem the slightest bit perturbed or unhappy about anything. No matter what is going on around him, he seems as serene as a monk. He barely knows a word of English but constantly speaks to us in Spanish as if we understand everything he is saying. I appreciate this, even if I haven't a clue.

We check into our rooms and our surfboards, as always, are waiting for us. They've been packed up and stored since our last trip. Tim can hardly wait to greet them.

He unzips his board bag and stares tenderly at his 7'2" blue buddy. He runs his hands over the rails.

"Go ahead," I say. "Head out, I know you can smell the water."

I don't have to suggest this twice. Tim is completely in his element here. The ocean is his chapel and he is ready for a revival.

He heads down to the beach and the kids and I unpack our things. Then Drew sinks into one of the hammocks down by the pool and Danielle and I take off for a walk.

There is something about the air here that gives me energy and calms me at the same time. I am completely at ease.

"You know, Danielle we could just open up our own little surf shop here and never go back."

"Mom, I would die of boredom. I mean, I like it here and all, but there's really nothing to do."

That is exactly what I love about this place. My life is never lacking in things to do. Sometimes the roar can just take over. Here the only roar is the ocean, and there is almost always laughter coming from somewhere.

"Hey Mom, remember Tim's Tidbits?"

"Oh yeah, that's right."

We decided on one of our past trips that Tim could just open up a little stand where he would give the surfcast every day. With thousands of obsessed surfers coming to Costa Rica's most consistent beach break, we figured we could make a fortune or at least enough to eat. His pearls of wisdom would be called Tim's Tidbits.

The sun is beginning its descent into the ocean as we all converge at a spot behind the hotel. This time of the day here always reminds me of that movie, "City of Angels." There's a scene in which all the angels one by one appear on the sand, drawn there at sunrise and sunset to hear heavenly strains of music. So it is here. One by one people appear here to pay homage to the day send it off into the night. Here the harmonies are color. Deep oranges, bright pink, magenta. All on a pallet of ever deepening blue.

"What a shock, Mom has her camera," Drew says.

I always take pictures of the sunset. At last count I had 317. They are all so beautiful. I don't want to miss capturing any of them. All I have to do is look at one of those pictures and I am instantly transported back to the peace I feel here.

I can almost hear the disk hiss as the tip of the florescent orange globe appears to touch the sea. The lower it sinks the more its colors are cast out around the sky. When the last of the fireball disappears beneath the horizon, Tim kisses me and offers a salute with his Imperial con limon, beer with lime.

"Que dia tan hermosa," Tim says. (*What a beautiful day*)

And so ends another day in paradise.

* * *

Our days here have passed so quickly I can hardly believe it is already time to leave for the rain forest.

My running has been the most pleasant surprise. I always run strong here. It probably has something to do with the fact that I am sleeping a solid 8 or 9 hours a night. I couldn't even dream about doing that at home. But between my healing ribs and my swollen feet, I haven't done a lot of running. If I get in a couple of days a week, I'm lucky. Here I have been able to run every day, at least five miles. I take off in the early morning, and just like at home, I hit the sand.

The sand here is much like it is in Jacksonville. Hard and packed at low tide. A perfect running surface. Not so unforgiving as the road, and yet firm enough for support. As the sun rises over the hills to the east the ocean is illuminated. The sea foam is as bright white as new snow and the waves reflect the light like a thousand small mirrors. Pelicans fly in formation low and slow over the water and rocks, and the tall sails of the schooner coming out of Tamarindo are striking against the severe blue of the Costa Rican sky. The faint smell of sweet smoke hangs in the air. It's the dry season, and miles away the park rangers are burning brush to keep the threat of wildfire down. Here, senses consumed, the miles have simply melted away beneath my feet. No pain at all. I am fully engulfed in the beauty of the moment.

Sandra is serving us breakfast this morning before we head out on the four hour trip to Arenal. I call her "mi hermana", my sister. From the moment we first met here several years ago, we had a definite connection of the spirit. If only we could communicate better. I suspect she speaks a bit more English than I do Spanish, but not much. We manage to get our messages across, but rarely without the aid of others.

I can tell she's worried about me. Like everyone else, she doesn't like to ask about the cancer, but I know it pains her.

"Too soon leaving," she says bunching her bottom lip into a pout.

"I know. One day I am going to come down here and just forget to go back."

"I have something for you," she says.

She sets a black plastic pyramid on the table in front of us, about three inches tall. Then fishes around in her apron pocket, lifting a second piece. It's a large purple, blue and white bird with long sweeping wings. She places the point of bird's beak on the very tip of the pyramid and lets go. The bird floats there, perfectly horizontal. Appears to defy gravity. Its body and wings suspended in air.

"That is freaky," says Drew. His eyes are almost as wide as the time I made him take the T-Rex ride at Disney.

"How is that possible?" he asks.

Sandra pats her mouth with her hand, searching for the right word.

Finally it comes to her.

"Balance," she says. "Just balance."

12 | Run to Daylight

January 19, 2008

It is so dark I can barely see my hand in front of my face. I feel for the button on the side of my watch that illuminates the time. 5:57 a.m.

"Tim, don't get too far ahead of me. I can't see a thing."

"Look to your left."

Tail lights flash in the parking lot of the Baldwin Rail Trail. I hear the muffled sound of voices nearby. Tim grabs my hand and we make our way toward the dozens of other runners gathering in the pre-dawn blackness. When our training runs get over 18 miles we come here. The old Baldwin CSX tracks have been converted into a trail for bikers and runners. Out and back is 28 miles of traffic free asphalt. Today we will only need 26.2 of those miles. This is it. The distance we've been working toward since we took our first steps back in July.

As we close in on the trailhead I can make out a few dim lights. Some of our Galloway group leaders have what I call miner hats on with small circular lights that shoot a beam of brightness in whatever direction they are looking. Others have red belt lights that strobe from the back of their running shorts. A few people have small flashlights.

There are signs up for each pacing group, but people are still milling around, chatting nervously about the distance, what they had for breakfast, how early they had to get up to get out here.

Then the booming voice of our co-group leader Chris Twiggs stops everyone in their tracks. Flashlights swing in his direction.

"Goood Morning Everyone! Are we ready for 26.2 miles?"

Whistles and hoots go up from the crowd.

"Remember when five miles seemed long? Well today folks when you step across this finish line, you will have reached one of the most impressive goals of your life. You will have done what less than one percent of the population can claim. You will be a marathoner. Amanda and I are very proud of all of you. Now make sure you find your group leader. Group leaders, hold your signs up high! Amanda, anything you want to add?"

"Only that if you are with the Renegades, The M&Ms or the F Squared Group, you are already way behind, because those groups decided to start at 5am so they could finish with everyone else," Amanda shouts.

Sometimes the slower groups like to start early on long run days. Usually everyone gets the message, but every now and then someone oversleeps or fails to get an email. No groans so Amanda continues.

"Sounds like we are good to go then. Let's head out. Fasties you go first. Sole Sisters, you're next. You all know your order. Have fun!"

One by one the groups begin to file, out fastest to slowest.

I fall in with Amanda's Sweet Feat group. We will all run out and back for 13 together. Then I'll wait at the finish line while they go back out for an additional 13.2. As we head down the trail, we are engulfed once again in darkness. I can't see my feet moving in front of me.

"The good thing about the dark is that we can't see the snakes." I recognize the voice of my fellow survivor, Kristi Pritchett.

"Oh, thanks for that, Kristi," I say. "That is just the mental picture I needed."

"Hey, Donna D! I'm so glad you are out here this mornin'. Are you going the whole way?"

"No, just half for me. Thirteen miles will be farther than I've run in a long time and more than likely I'll do the half marathon on race day."

"More than likely? Does that mean you are leaving the door open to do the full?"

"Oh, I doubt that. I just can't bring myself to completely rule it out, you know?"

"Yes, I know where you're coming from."

"I know you do. How are you doing?"

"Oh, I'm fine. I'm fine. Just getting geared up to start chemo."

"Do you have to start before the race?"

"Yeah, I have my first treatment on Monday, but it's the only one I'll have to have before the marathon, so I think I'll have plenty of time to recover."

Kristi first started running with us in July to honor her sister Jan who is a breast cancer survivor.

Then, in November, just three months before our inaugural race, she was diagnosed with the disease. She had a lumpectomy a month ago and now here she is running 26 miles. The marathon itself will be on her birthday.

"You know Kristi, you've got to stop copying me," I tease.

"Yeah, well you know that's my goal in life. I want to be just like you, only taller," she laughs.

"Walk break!"

Every three minutes Amanda calls the walk break. This is how our Galloway run/walk/run training works. We are divided up in to groups based on our speed. Tim's group is the fastest. They run for five minutes and walk for 40 seconds. My group does three and ones. Run for three minutes, walk for one. We are middle of the packers. Even the walkers put in what Jeff calls shuffle breaks. The idea is to change up the muscle groups that you are using to reduce fatigue, lessen injury and leave more power for the late miles of the race.

Tim and I were both skeptical about this at first. Both of us always liked to run without stopping, and there's a bit of the ego involved as well. Still, the results speak for themselves. After almost a dozen years of times that weren't good enough to qualify for Boston, Tim has now qualified two years in a row using the Galloway method. He finds that the extra rest his legs get just makes him faster when the other runners are starting to cramp up around mile 20. Since we started with the group, he consistently has negative splits in his long races, meaning basically that he gets faster as he goes along. It all may seem counter intuitive but it works. I can't say that I've gotten any faster, but I have certainly remained far more injury free. After all my body has been through, for the time being at least, I am just happy to be out here running.

I coast up to where Amanda is leading the group.

"How are we coming on the FAQ page on the website?"

Amanda is used to beginning conversations with me in mid thought. We talk so many times each day now that there is really no need for hellos. She is spearheading our website design and now that we are getting down to the wire, the updates are coming fast and furious. We've been batting around a frequently asked questions page for a couple of weeks now.

"Should be up on Monday. I also just updated the Why I'm Running Page. You have got to check that out. There's so much great stuff coming in."

"I'll do it this afternoon."

"Bring your tissues, girlfriend."

We march on in silence for a while, the sound of our feet like gently falling rain on the pavement. Running with the group makes the miles disappear almost without notice. Even when no words are spoken, sometimes especially then, the camaraderie we feel lifts us up and carries us along.

At 6:45 we see the first hint of the sunrise to come.

I feel good. In fact, really good.

Wonder if I should just run the whole way?

By 7:15 the trail is in full view, as are the trees and the few homes dotting the rural landscape around us. Roosters patrol a yard here and there, announcing the new day, and rebel flags are more common than the stars and stripes. Occasionally, shots ring out from a nearby shooting range. Signs tell us the gunfire sounds closer than it is, but it's unsettling when it happens.

Footsteps are coming up fast behind me.

"Help!"

I turn to see Ike streaking up beside me. Ike is African American. The images are too much for him to resist. He looks down at me in mock terror, his eyes wide as saucers.

"Don't you leave me alone out here Miss Donna. They'll never find me."

"No worries, Ike. You stay right here with me. I'll protect you."

Someone in the back of the pack starts mimicking the music from the movie *Deliverance* and laughter pierces the morning air.

"That's six and a half miles, ladies and gentlemen, time to turn," Amanda announces.

The remaining six and a half miles evaporate into the growing light.

I step across the finish line wishing for more.

"OK, don't get comfortable folks. We still have a half marathon to run. Grab some water and let's head back out," Amanda shouts.

I could run back out with them, and if I get tired I'll just use my cell phone to call Tim and he can come get me.

I catch Kristi's eye. She knows what I'm thinking.

"I'll put the miles in for both of us today, alright?"

She's right. I could run farther, but there is a world of difference between 13.1 and 26.2. Even on my strongest day, a marathon is a challenge.

"Sounds like a plan. I'll be waiting for you all right here."

As each team and its members cross the finish line, I hand out Galloway medals signifying the completion of the training. I love watching the faces of the finishers. If I am honest, I would prefer to be one of them. But it is priceless to watch a first time marathoner go the distance. The sense of pride and accomplishment is evident in the smiles and tears of each elated and exhausted runner.

It's a party now. One of our group leaders, Carolyn Graham, has arranged a feast for us in the parking lot.

In the last tenth of a mile the runners can smell the food and the finish line.

Kristi bounds across the line looking as fresh as she did five hours ago. All of the teams who have finished earlier are there cheering.

"Woo hoo!! Looking great! Way to go!"

It's an emotional scene. There watching with the rest of us is Kristi's friend Todd Smith. He has been here for hours holding a dozen pink roses anxiously waiting to congratulate her. Kristi is beaming. Standing there with her roses and her medal she looks like she just won the Miss America pageant.

"You just need a crown," I say, pulling her into a hug.

"How sweet is that?" she says looking at Todd.

"Well you deserve it girl! But I have to say you look too good for a woman who just ran 26 miles. Are you sure you didn't just hide in a bush and run in with everyone," I say.

"I feel great. It was awesome, Donna. Just awesome. And you know I appreciate it so much because of everything that's going on right now."

Kristi is far from alone. Many of our runners have their own very compelling reasons for joining our journey. Some are survivors. Others are supporting family or friends with breast cancer. In the afternoon I settle in to get to know some of them. Honestly, I don't do this often. I should, but it all just hits so close to home. Some days I have the strength, other days I don't. I open my laptop and click the link to the Why I'm Running page on the breastcancermarathon.com website. As Amanda suggested, a box of tissues is on the table beside me.

Why I'm running

My wife is a 5 year breast cancer survivor. I am extremely proud of her efforts and accomplishments over these past 5 years. I, on the other hand have let her down a number of times during the last 10 years. In February I came within "pills" of committing suicide. Things that saved me were the constant flashbacks of my family from the past 27 years. My wife and 3 kids' faces actually gave me the strength to discard those pills and walk away alive! I have recently begun running, again. The last time I enjoyed running was when I was in prison, during 10/99 and 3/01. I was in a federal camp for a white collar crime. But none the less it was still prison. Running gave me a sense of freedom, accomplishment, satisfaction and motivation. So I decided to begin again. I am 52 years old and in what I feel is relatively good shape compared to many others I am around. I plan on doing a 5K run toward the end of July, then a 8K run in September, maybe a half-marathon this fall and then your marathon next year. I intend to fund raise my way to Florida with also a big donation! God willing I will make it there to help "all" breast cancer victims and to a lesser degree, myself. Thank you for your time, I hope someone reads this…

John

> > > >

Dear Donna

My reason for running. My sister in law, she is a survivor for 8 years. She is now going through test for possible recurrence. Let's all pray it's not there. I also have 3 new sisters, our parents married last June. They are wonderful women. They lost their mother to breast cancer. Anyway I want to pay tribute to these two women by completing this run. Run, walk or crawl - I will finish!!!

Daryl Owen

> > > >

My sister found a lump in April, and now we are fighting back with chemo, faith & lots of laughter. If she hadn't done her own BSE, her prognosis could be so different. I run so that every woman remembers … TOUCH

YOURSELF! I run so that women like my sister Cheena can keep their taste buds, and their hair. I run to combat the fear my two beautiful nieces have in their hearts for the life of their mother, and for their future. I run for my husband, who loves me enough to put pink ribbons on my calendars each month. I run for the 1 in 8 to someday be 1 in 8,000,000. I run for all of you, because nobody knows strength more intimately than a survivor, and if one step can bring courage or encouragement to you, then I should run a million miles for your honor and for your life.

Joynicole Martinez

Rocky Mount, NC

> > > >

I have decided to participate in the National Breast Cancer Marathon under Team Genentech. I am dedicating my run to a very special group of ladies from Bakersfield California who call themselves the HER2 Sisterhood. They are breast cancer survivors who have HER2 positive breast cancer and who have received Herceptin, some for several years. They are not defined by their cancer. They dedicate their time to help others navigate through their journey with HER2 positive breast cancer. They are inspiring. They are strong. They are survivors. I have not had breast cancer and no one in my family has either but I am inspired by these women daily. I am blessed to work for a company that puts the patient FIRST!! Here's to my Bakersfield girls!!

Lori Lanphere

> > > >

My Mom was only 18 years old when she was diagnosed with breast cancer. She went through the surgery and treatment alone. She exemplified what it meant to be a true survivor. I don't want to be scared and I don't want to be a survivor. I am running so there will be a cure. I am proud to say that I will be running in my Mom's honor, not her memory. My Mom is now a 37 year survivor!

Jennifer Lambert

> > > >

Hi. Last year, I was attempting to run 60 marathons. I made it to 36: I had to stop in August when a family member was diagnosed with breast cancer and I stopped to take care of her. Believe me, we know about "living with breast cancer" now.

She is doing well, and I am running again. I have decided that I want to run 50 to 60 marathons around the US between 1/8/07 and 2/17/08 in her honor. The final one would be, of course, the National Marathon to Fight Breast Cancer.

Robert Lopez

Marathon Maniac #111

> > > >

Hi Donna

You've changed my life.

I bet you hear that a lot, in fact, I'm sure you do, because I've read the same thing written by hundreds of people in your book. But, I thought you deserved to hear it again. I'm not a runner. Maybe soon, I will be. Since January I've been training for your race. I'll be joined by some of my more experienced friends soon, and then we all start training for real in August. I'm going to need ever day from now until then to build up my base, but I am more determined than I have ever been in my entire life to do just that. I've had one goal for the past two or three months, and it's been to finish your marathon.

My friends mother was recently diagnosed with Breast Cancer. Friends and I planned to run a 5k for breast cancer in her name, but it just didn't seem powerful enough. We wanted, as you said,"a long arduous race that challenges the body, mind, and spirit."We decided that if we're going to do anything at all, we might as well Go Big or Go Home. On my runs, when it feels as though I can't take another step, I think of my friend's mother. Every day, she is fighting for her life. Suddenly, it's easier to put one foot in front of the other again. As she fights the cancer, I fight the pain in my legs, and that little voice in my head that says I can't go any farther. Your race has allowed me to stand with her, fighting my fight because I can't fight hers. So for that, I thank you. You have given me an incredible gift, the opportunity to believe in myself and fight for a cause. I'll make you proud on race day! I've created a training website for my team in order to chronicle our progress and help us with our ambitious fundraising goal.

Thanks so much,

Jeff "Dubbs"

> > > >

While there are so many women who have battled Breast Cancer, I feel drawn to run for one person in particular. She is an amazing person, with baby blue eyes, freckles across her nose, and a smile that will melt your heart. This amazing person is my beautiful 8 year old Natalie.

She dreams of one day being the zookeeper in charge of the Jacksonville zoo, of saving the earth, and of one day becoming a mommy. I run so that hopefully she will never have to worry about Breast Cancer, so that she can live her life chasing her dreams instead of worrying about a lump in her breast. I run because I never want her to have to fight this horrible disease like so many others have had to do. So for my darling daughter, and all of the little girls out there, I run for your future.

Rebecca Manning

> > > >

Many people don't understand why people run marathons. I have done other races to stay active and to achieve goals that I have set for myself. This marathon however is different on so many levels. Training for this is not just a way for me to stay fit. I am running in honor of my Aunt Eileen, a 10 year survivor. I am running to show her how thankful I am to have her in my life. I am running to show her that I am proud of her for being a survivor. Training in Chicago, in the middle of winter, has been a challenge. Each time I train, I remember what my aunt went through to be a "winner". I know that my grueling workouts are nothing compared to the challenge she has been through. To my auntie and godmother, I love you and will be thinking of you the entire 26.2 miles!

Megan Weber

> > > >

I am running to honor the memory of my sweet wife, Claudia Ann Davis, who died last July 23, 2007 following a 20-month battle with breast cancer. Claudia was a runner herself, but she was so much more; a supporter and encourager for me. Even if she were not running a particular race, she would always be there to encourage me. Even during her illness, she would travel with me, sitting in the car and when I passed she would get out, take my picture and give me a big kiss to strengthen me. I miss her so much, but realize that she would want more than anything for me to continue, for she was so proud of my running. I know now that she is not suffering anymore, and she always supported any and all of the efforts to fund breast cancer research. Running in this marathon is something that I can do to continue her efforts. I am proud to run this marathon with Donna to help find a cure for this terrible disease. I'm "taking Claudia with me" as I run this marathon, for I run in a shirt with her picture on the back.

David Davis

> > > >

I picture what David's wife might look like. Claudia smiling from the picture on the back of his shirt.

Closing the page, I leave the website, collect the pile of crumpled tissues next to my computer and toss them in the trash.

How many tissues did the authors of these stories go through as they wrote?

There is so much pain in these stories. So much courage. So many people fighting. But there is hope too.

What will it be like when all of these people are at the start line next month? All of that hope, and courage and pain and energy in one place. All of those stories connected by the heart that it takes to be a marathoner.

A chill of excitement runs through my body. I can already feel the electricity along the course.

I'm just about to turn off my computer and call it a day when the chime sounds indicating I have a new e-mail. It's from my friend Rik Schellenberg. An update on his wife Laurie who has been battling breast cancer for a long time. A group of us have been on his mailing list through several years of ups and downs.

Dear friends and family,

Our sister in law, Suzanne, offered to compose an update for Laurie to send to you (see attachment). So, here it is! Thank you for all your well wishes, prayers and acts of kindness.

We love you,

Rik and Laurie

Saturday afternoon (January 19, 2008)

Dear Family and Friends,

Laurie is home again (Jan. 17) from a short stay in the hospital this week to relieve a fever and reduce spiked bilirubin, for which the doctors added a third external drain.

She is up and around making visits to the family room and kitchen to visit when she's not resting.

She has improved appetite eating some favorite foods-Wendy's Frostys and baked potatoes, homemade soups, and even some bites of pizza last night (hard to resist pizza!)

Home health care makes visits 3 times a week to educate and administer to the drains. Laurie has also requested a physical therapy evaluation to perhaps receive some massage therapy (I think both Rik and sister, Pam, are hoping for reinforcements?). There continues to be some irritating lower back pain thus the desire for massage.

With the help of neighbors and family, Evie has been carrying on her normal play activities over the last several days with only the energy that a 5 year old has. T.D. is doing well with school and his intramural team won another basketball game today (last Sat. too).

Today (Saturday) the whole Davis clan (Laurie's sisters, their spouses, nieces and great niece) was in town answering telephones and greeting well wishers at the door. As the sisters admirably described the neighborhood-it's like living in Mayberry RFD. Everyone really looks after each other (minus the town drunk and Barney the bumbling deputy of course).

This coming Monday Laurie's long time hair designer, Douglas, will pay a house call to give her a hair cut/blow dry-we girls know what a lift that is (I'm not trying to leave the guys out. Do the guys experience that same thing when they go to the barber?)!

Tuesday, Laurie will go to Mayo for lab tests to check her progress and meet with her doctor.

Continue to pray for improved test results.

After the national holiday on Monday requests for afternoon help with Evie continue as Laurie regains strength.

Please reply via email if you are able to help.

United in prayer,

Suzanne (Schellenberg)

Well, that doesn't sound good.

I stare at the page for a moment, then take a deep breath and close my computer.

I should write back. But not now.

Suddenly the physical and mental exercises of the day are weighing on my eyelids. Tim and I got up this morning at 4 a.m. He's been sleeping with a book on his chest for about an hour. I climb into bed next to him and tuck myself under his arm. I need to feel the warmth of his body. The rhythm of his breathing soothes me and I escape into the darkness of a dreamless sleep.

13 | Top to Bottom

February 9, 2008

Tim peeks over his reading glasses at me. He is standing in his usual spot. The side of the kitchen counter serves as his desk in the morning. My obsessively organized husband is going over our schedule for the day.

"We should be going in about ten minutes," he says.

I am still sitting at the kitchen table with my robe on.

"I know."

Still I don't move.

"Big day, huh?"

"Plenty to do, that's for sure. What time is everything again?"

Tim passes his notepad to me.

7 am – Final 7 mile run with team

9 am - San Jose Episcopal Day School Kids Marathon

11 am – Tim Surf???

Noon- Drew's Basketball Game

2pm – Laurie Schellenberg's Funeral

4pm - Danielle's Volleyball Tournament

"Can we add 8pm go to bed and sleep for 12 hours?"

"We can." Tim walks over and puts his hands on my shoulders.

They are warm, reassuring.

"We'll get there. Just take one thing at a time. The run will be a fun celebration. It's short. People will be looking for your energy today."

"I know, and the momentum is just so strong for the race right now. I will enjoy sharing that."

"You will if you make it to the run. Unless you are planning to do 7 miles in that robe, you need to get dressed. We need to get going."

"Maybe I will wear it. This robe is very comfortable."

Tim can't stand to be late. Ever. You can set your watch by him. I on the other hand am almost always late. When we go places together, I do my best not to ruin his reputation.

I hurry into my running shorts and tank and grab my socks and shoes.

"OK, surfer boy, let's go. I can put on my shoes in the car. At least we're close."

The final run of the training season is just blocks away in Atlantic Beach. We are meeting at the One Ocean Resort, formerly known as the Sea Turtle Inn. The resort was supposed to be remodeled in time to be our host hotel, but construction has been running behind.

We arrive at the hotel parking lot to see piles of construction materials still strewn everywhere.

Everyone is there ready to go. Chris and Amanda are already making some final announcements. This will be the last time we are all together before the marathon next weekend.

"I see Donna and Tim have arrived," Chris says.

Tim shoots me a look. It is two minutes after 7.

"Any final words for the team, Donna?"

Chris is standing on the bed of a truck so everyone can see him.

"Help me up there would you, Chris?"

He reaches for my hand and pulls me onto the truck. The atmosphere is electric with anticipation of what's to come next week. I look out at the faces of the friends who have become more like family to me over the months and in some cases years we've trained together.

There's Mary Binkley, the perky blonde with the thick southern accent who gathered her friends to pray with me when I got the last diagnosis. The first time I ever interviewed Mary as part of my weekly television journal, I asked her why she was running. I'm not sure exactly what she meant to say, but what came out was "it is important for our bosoms to feel good." I still tease her about this.

And I see Phil Clark, a tall dark police officer who seems about twice my height. Phil always has a smile on his face and regularly gets up two hours before the rest of us with Chris and Amanda to set out coolers along the training course. He has a booming voice that belies his very thin frame so we often call on his volume to round up the runners. After all this time, it's still hard for me to believe that voice comes out of that body.

There's Dawn Hagel, another group leader, who has more energy than ten people put together. Dawn has long silky brown hair that she usually pulls back into a pony tail and she is never lacking for the next great idea for fundraising. She is almost singlehandedly coordinating a silent auction for the marathon to benefit The Donna Foundation.

Kurtis Loftus is there. He's our Peter Pan. His blue eyes sparkle when he talks, and he has a boyish enthusiasm for everything. Kurtis and his daughter attend every Jaguars football game together and as a graphic artist, he has come up with some unique items to bring to the stadium. He got his picture in the paper one day with a little contraption he calls "the Jag Hammer". It's a Jaguar head helmet with a large cardboard jack hammer towering over the top that he created and wears in the stands. Kurtis is going to have fun no matter what he's doing. He keeps a weekly blog called 26.Gulp that chronicles our Saturday training runs. In addition to designing the medals and our race poster he has created the most beautiful art work from sketches done during our runs. He's selling them as a way to raise money for the cause as well.

And there is Jim Gilmore grinning up at me. He leads our "Gliders" group. Jim is tall, not Phil tall, but at least six feet, and blonde with black "Clark Kent" glasses framing his face. That's appropriate because Jim is my Superman.

A developer by trade, he was the first person I went to when I knew I'd need to garner city support for the marathon. All I really knew about Jim other than his professional success at helping to redevelop the beaches, was that he had connections on the Chamber of Commerce. Asking for his help is the best decision I could have ever made. Jim likes to fly under the radar, but the truth is he knows everyone. Beyond Edith and Jeff, he has been the engine driving our inaugural success so far. He connected me with Theresa Price and her unparalleled team at the Office of Special Events, helped us get a tourism development grant to get started, negotiated big deals with sponsors, and most importantly believed in me and my vision. He is one of the busiest people I know, but whenever I ask him to do "one more thing for me" he always says yes. He watches my back. I trust him with my life. Jim is literally the brother I never had.

I love these people. They have made this journey such a joy. I can't wait to share the success of our first race with them.

"What a year it's been everyone and what a wonderful journey we have all taken together. You are all very special to me. I know you are feeling the same sense of pride, accomplishment and anticipation that I am about the race next week. We could have never done any of this without you," I begin.

Shouts of excitement and applause punctuate my words.

"I have some new numbers for you. With seven days to go, we are now over $650,000 raised and 6000 runners. We have already far exceeded anyone's expectations for this inaugural year, and registrations are still coming in fast and furious. Fundraising alone is already at more than $300,000 dollars and climbing by the minute!"

The cheers are now so loud that I worry we are going to violate the morning noise ordinance for Atlantic Beach.

"The route we are running this morning will take us directly along part of the marathon course. So soak it in. It's been ours for a long time, and now we're going to share it with thousands of others. Imagine what it will look like when it is lined with cheering people and all of us have one goal, to finish breast cancer. I get chills just thinking about it. I wish there was some way we could all run every step together, but in a very significant way that is exactly what we are doing. Enjoy each other out there today and I'll see you at the starting line next Sunday!"

More applause and Chris returns to the truck.

"It wouldn't be a training run without some final words of advice and guidance from Dr. John," he says, motioning for John to come up and speak.

In addition to being the leader of our walking group, "The Lovers", Dr. John has been a coach with the Galloway program for longer than most of us have been running. He's an icon. He's been living with Leukemia for a number of years now but rarely misses a Saturday training run. He's also a smart ass from the word go and the king of the tasteless joke. This is his charm.

"OK, listen up," he says. "This is important. I've been getting the same question over and over again about next Sunday. The question many of you are asking is this. 'Is it OK to have sex before the race?' The answer is *Yes*, of course it is!"

He pauses for effect.

"Just make sure you don't distract the race officials."

"OOOOH." Groans and scattered laughter spread through the crowd as Chris tells everyone to take off.

"I understand you can't stay for the entire run today," Chris says to me.

"No, I'll do five or so. Then I've got to shower and get across town for the kids' run."

"OK, have fun. I'm so excited I don't know how I'm going to wait another week."

"Me too."

I give Chris a long hug. He and Amanda ultimately are the rudders that steer our ship week in and week out in training. With their dark hair and brown eyes, they look like they could be brother and sister. To our runners, they are the head of the family. Chris leaves us every summer to run an ultra-marathon called The Hard Rock 100 in the San Juan Mountains of southwest Colorado. This gives Amanda some bonding time with the team. When he comes back she will take a week or two, and then they are both there every week for the rest of the six months of training. It's a ton of work, and if we arrive at 6 a.m. they are there at 4 a.m. In the years I've known them I have never heard a negative word from either.

"Thanks for everything, man. This is going to be great," I say and take off to catch the crowd.

With each step I run I can feel my body relaxing. The salt air, the sweat. The companionship. By the time I meet Tim at the car I'm feeling more equipped to face the day. He turns to me with a smile.

"Good run?"

"Is there any other kind?"

We drive home, rinse off, and we are on to our next destination. Valerie Brown, who has been helping Jim put our marathon sponsorships together, greets us at the track at Dupont Middle School, where the kids' race is taking place. Her daughter will be among those running.

"I'm so glad you could make it," she says excitedly. "This just means everything to the kids."

I look over her shoulder stunned at the scene in front of me.

"Wow."

"I know," Val says. "They really went all out."

The stands are full. There are decorations, and bands, and cheerleaders and banners everywhere.

Dozens of pink clad runners are stretching, getting ready for their final laps. These San Jose Episcopal Day School students have trained for their own version of the marathon for 26 weeks. The 6th graders have been running a mile a week since early fall to make sure they get enough miles in to run their 26th today. As they get ready to begin, The fourth graders file onto risers and begin playing the song "Low Rider" on recorders.

A teacher announces our presence and the children roar their appreciation.

"OK, everyone now that our special guests are here, let's get ready to run," she shouts.

The kids cue up at the start line. Tim lines up next to them. A bunch of little girls point and giggle. Tim often gets this reaction from women whether they are 12 or 42.

"It's Tim Deeeegan," one of them squeals.

Parents are in the stands holding signs of support and waving pink pompoms. Tweeeeeet!

The whistle sounds and gangly legs go flying everywhere. Some children look as if they could run forever. Others are clearly at their limits but everyone is smiling and laughing.

Tim runs at various paces making sure he jogs along with each group of kids for just a little while. I'm snapping pictures and high fiving the runners as they make their way around the track. One lap, two, three, and the fourth lap makes a mile!

When they finish I place a medal around each person's neck and pronounce them "marathoners".

Now it's a party.

A band of teachers and parents strikes up the tune "I Will Survive" on pink guitars. A number of survivors are honored, and I am presented with a bouquet of pink roses with pink notes attached inside. I pluck one from the bunch.

"Thanks for teaching us that there is hope even when you think things are hopeless," it says. I tuck the note back into the flowers and swallow hard. It is a touching display. Leave it to kids to get it right. Looking at these fresh faces I feel a rush of optimism about the future.

"I'm so glad we came," I tell Tim as we walk toward to car.

"Me too. It's great to see kids moving their bodies. The earlier the better."

"And they are already snapping on how great it feels to do something for others. It's a win-win all around."

"Can you believe those kids are only a year younger than Drew?" Tim asks.

I look back at them one last time. Most are tiny, still children. They are just at the beginning of middle school. These are the years when suddenly kids transition from child to teen. By 7th and 8th grade they'll be four or five inches taller with voices an octave lower.

That's what happened to my Drew. It all seemed to occur in one day, I dialed his cell phone and a voice I barely recognized answered the phone. Pow! Your child is gone, and he's been replaced with a young man. In fact the whole transition has just happened in the last few months. For the longest time I saved an old phone message from him, just so I could still have my little boy.

"Drew looked just like them last year," I say. "I was taller than him when he was in 6th grade. Now he's passed me by five inches."

Drew just turned 13 and he is 13 in every sense of the word. Every now and then I still see his wicked cute grin turned my way, but mostly I'm not too smart anymore and I'm no longer the person he wants to shoot hoops with. Some days it breaks my heart. But I know it's a phase. We'll get through it together.

"Remember when he swore he would never like girls or broccoli and I made him write it down and sign it like a contract? I still have it, you know."

"Well, he's still holding strong on the broccoli part," Tim observes.

Back at home Tim grabs a quick surf session. The water is cold so it's literally only a couple of waves just to touch the water. How that man jumps in the water in February without a wet suit I will never know.

"It's invigorating," he says, as he pads into the house with his board.

"Uh-huh, well now that you are invigorated, let's catch some basketball."

The gym at St. Paul's Catholic School is just down the street. This is league play. The off-season club that gets the boys ready for next year's school team.

As we walk in I wave at Drew and get a small acknowledgement. I'll take it.

The game itself looks more like a rugby match than a basketball game.

"They are so rough," I say to Tim.

"That's how they play the game now," Tim says. "Very physical."

Drew hits a beautiful three pointer.

"Woo hoo, way to go Drew!" I am a serious screamer at my kids' games. I think it embarrasses them sometimes but I don't care. They would never admit it, but I suspect at least a little part of them likes it. Watching them play, whether it's basketball, baseball, volleyball or piano, is all pure joy to me. I'm hoping to store up some of that for the next stop on the day's hectic schedule.

Laurie Schellengberg's funeral has been sitting there like a stone weighing on my brain for days.

As we once again cross the city, making our way to St. Joseph's Catholic

Church for the service, my mind is retracing the events of the past week.

An email from Rik, basically a concession that we were going to lose Laurie, was a sock in the gut. Laurie was a patient at Mayo too so I knew Edith was familiar with her case. I forwarded Rik's email to her, along with an angry note from me.

From: Donna Deegan

Sent: Thursday, January 31, 2008 12:43 AM

To: Perez, Edith A., M.D.

Subject: FW: Update on Laurie

I'm sure you probably know about this. This is my friend that you saw at Julie's party at Christmas. I can't stop crying. I'm just so tired of losing people and so scared. This is why I am always looking for other things that might make a difference Edith. For all of your wonderful work, we are still losing. Medicine can only seemingly stem the tide, not turn it. This woman has a five year old child with Down Syndrome. What is she going to do without a mother? It makes me so angry!

> > > >

From: Rik Schellenberg

Sent: Wednesday, January 30, 2008 9:06 PM

Subject: Update on Laurie

All – I wanted to first take this opportunity to thank everyone for your thoughts and prayers for Laurie's health. We have been blessed with incredible support from family, friends and strangers. The love, prayers and support are heartfelt and greatly appreciated.

Laurie came home on Thursday, January 17th. We had a brief stay at St.

Luke's Hospital on Monday the 21st due to another infection. The physicians added a 3rd drain which has eliminated visits back to the hospital.

She's enjoying the company of her sisters (and guests) especially the back massages/rubs from family and friends. She tries to join us for dinner just so she can play the game of the night –, "Know Your Country", "Know Your Animals (like, what animal has a ring tail . . . a ring-tailed lemur, of course) or the "Who" game.

Her last visit to her Oncologist was last Tuesday – the biliruben has stabilized but has not fallen to an acceptable level for continued chemotherapy. As such, we have accepted the services of Hospice – they are a fantastic organization. From the first day of their visit (last Thursday), we have been cared for and our requests have been met. An assigned nurse, social worker and a home care assistant are some of the services provided by hospice.

The medication has helped eased the pain but it causes her to be very sleepy. She is constantly nauseous which has been attributed to the cancer involvement in the liver. We are trying to come up with the right balance of meds to ease that discomfort.

We are working diligently on finding a sitter for Evie during the weekdays (between 3:00 and 6:00) and some Saturdays. Thank you to those who have offered your time and home – we may still reach out to you but our hope is to have some consistency in her care with a permanent sitter/nanny.

I wish I could share more positive news for you. She is an amazing woman with great inner strength and strong faith in God. It is in His hand.

Please continue your prayers!

Edith's response had been that of a woman who has seen much, and invested even more.

From: Perez, Edith MD

Sent: January 31, 2008 9:35 AM

Subject: Re: Update on Laurie

Some days can truly be challenging . . . trust me when I say I understand . . . When this happens it does take a toll, as one can think why try so hard? But somehow, in the depths of our souls and brains we have to keep trying . . .

Keep trying. Keep pushing the boulder up the hill. That's what it feels like to me.

Tim and I enter the church and take a pew along the right side. Then I notice Aurora Weiss, the Spanish whirlwind who volunteers on the chemo floor at Mayo. Aurora has been living with a vicious cancer called Multiple Myeloma for almost 16 years. They gave her maybe a year when she was diagnosed. She told them they were nuts, and went on with her life. She reminds me of Susan. She's been through every awful body draining treatment in the world but she is the happiest person alive. Her light illuminates the 8th floor and every patient she touches. What a strong spirit. Right now though, hers seems as broken as mine. I slip out of my pew, make my way toward the front and slide in next to her. She is in tears.

"I loved her so much," she says, dabbing her eyes with a tissue.

"I know." I pull her into an embrace and we hold each other tightly, not wanting to let go.

Rik walks down the middle aisle holding his daughter Evie's hand. He looks soaked in sadness from the inside out. I have known Rik since the 5th grade. He was always the class clown. It's been a while since I've seen him smile.

A few days ago I went with Susie Slappey, another childhood friend and the treasurer of my foundation, to see Laurie one last time. True to form, she had spent the last days of her life organizing the household needs so that Rik would be able to handle things after she was gone. I brought her a special rosary my friend Ernie Bono had given me that had been blessed by the Catholic Saint Padre Pio. His instructions had been to keep it until someone else needed it more. Laurie was that someone. I also gave her a pair of pink earrings, with a matching set for Evie. She seemed thrilled, and completely at peace with whatever was to come.

"I've done what I can, Donna. I'm just giving it all to God," she said.

I wasn't ready to let it go.

"Laurie, are you sure you don't want another opinion? I am starting to look into some holistic things."

"I'm open to anything, Donna. Don't get me wrong. I still have a lot of hope," she said.

Rik sat there rubbing her shoulders and listening. He was completely together until we walked outside. Then all the pain he'd been holding in came rushing out.

I held him as he cried.

"I don't know what to do anymore, Donna. One minute she seems resigned to dying and then she says something like she just said to you. What more can we do?"

"I don't know, Rik, but I'll work on finding out. If she isn't ready to say that's it, we should see if there are other options."

Laurie died a couple of days later.

In retrospect, I think I was the only one who wasn't ready.

I'm still not. This is just too much to accept.

I give Aurora's hand a last squeeze and go back to my place next to Tim.

The music plays. Father Cody talks about a loving mother and faithful servant. I am gritting my teeth so hard that my jaw is starting to ache. I can't take my eyes off Rik and his kids. When the service is over, I exchange a few words with friends and make a bee line for the car. Rik catches me as we approach the exit.

"You doing OK?" he asks.

"Am I doing OK?"

"You still have a lot of work to do Donna. Don't ever stop. You keep working until we find a cure. We can't get there fast enough."

Certainly not fast enough for Laurie. At the moment this is all I can see and I let the anger engulf me.

I am barely breathing. Barely allowing myself to breathe. I'm afraid if I do, I'll start to cry and I'll never stop. Why do I deserve to breathe anyway? She can't. Laurie isn't breathing anymore. I just saw her at Christmas and now she's gone. Just saw her looking healthy and stunning in a little black dress. I can still see her smile from across the room. Her perfect white teeth against her tan skin. Her eyes twinkling as she sips a glass of red wine. Beautiful at Christmas. Dead by Valentine's Day. I can't get the insanity of that out of my head.

She has little children for God's sake! What about Evie? And T.D. He is only 12. In 7th grade like Drew. Such a vulnerable age for a boy. He needs his mother!

The rage is rising from my gut like vomit and I am ready to hurl it out like a fast ball at God.

Damn it! I am so sick of you taking people too soon! Sick of your disregard for the lives they still need to lead. Sick of the fear and the pain and the chaos. Where's the mercy? Why are these kids left without a mother? Why should Rik have to live without the love of his life?

I don't expect any answers. My head is screaming too loudly to hear them anyway.

Tim glances over at me from behind the wheel. I am chewing my top lip with a vengeance. A nervous habit I fall into whenever I am trying desperately not to lose it. He says nothing. He knows better. Tim always has to defend God and I am in no mood to hear it.

My mind is racing, looking for a release that won't come.

Get it together, Donna. You need to be there for Danielle.

I still have a volleyball game to attend and we will have to go straight there. We drive silently to the gym at The Bolles School where the tournament is taking place.

I spot Danielle's curly ponytail bouncing in the distance. Then she spots me. She smiles and waves and the team continues to warm up. This alone is normally all it takes to send my heart sailing, but right now I have no wind. Usually I can tell you every move my daughter makes on the court. Every set, every serve. I'm the annoying parent who is constantly circling the court clicking away on my camera, blinding everyone with my oversized flash. But today I am barely holding on. I am determined not to lose it in front of her so I disconnect. She is here but I am not.

Finally in the privacy of my home I close the door behind me. I let one furious thought replace the next. The more I think about the injustice of Laurie's death, the greater my anger and frustration become. I pace the room until my eyes catch a picture sitting on the piano. Danielle and Drew smiling back at me from the frame. Inside my own four walls, the mask comes off and my heart breaks wide open. The breath I have been holding explodes from my chest in sobs that come hard and unrelenting.

I am so tired. So tired of being afraid. So tired of being brave. I have been running for so long. But just like in a dream, I can't run fast enough to get away. I can pull away for short periods of time or not look back. But I can never just leave it in the dust. I am running the wheel and fear is always right behind me and right before me.

14 | Convergence Aloft

February 11, 2008

Iffy. I don't like the word at all. Especially when it comes to the weather forecast the week of the race. Yet that is what I'm hearing from my meteorologist/co-anchor husband.

Sitting on our large mango colored couch, I'm about to squeeze the life out of an oversized blue accent pillow. There is nothing indecisive about the colors in our home. Bold shades of orange, yellow, and bright blue are everywhere.

"What do you mean, iffy?" I ask.

"Just what I said, Donna. Listen, I don't make the weather. I just try to predict it."

Tim sweeps his hand through his sun bleached hair. He does this whenever he's trying to give himself time to respond without sounding irritated.

"We are still a week out. You know things will change, but I can only tell you what the models are saying."

What they are saying is that we have a beautiful week ahead, but that a major front is going to move in on race weekend. Right now it looks like it will hold off until after the race, but it's going to be close.

"Tim, I've been planning this race for more than two years. I need good weather."

My eyes bore a hole into his. I make no attempt to hide my irritation. I know it is not rational to blame my husband for the weather.

So what!

"Would you prefer I keep the forecast from you? Or make one up?"

He cocks his head and his eye brows rise at the question.

My inner brat retreats.

"Of course not," I say, backing down from the ledge. "I know I can only control what I can control. I just want things to be perfect."

Tim takes a deep breath. The lines on his forehead soften.

"I know. Well, I don't think you should worry. Didn't you put Susan in charge of the weather?"

"Good point."

Susan. The memory of that conversation makes me smile. Susan died last year in the midst of our planning. My indestructible friend who lived so many years longer than the doctors thought was possible. She was utterly fearless.

"I'm not afraid at all," she told me. "I'm just going to miss everyone. But it doesn't mean I can't help with the marathon. I'll just be in charge of the weather."

OK girl, work your magic. I need you.

"All right, weatherman I'm off your case," I say, doing my best to lighten up.

No meteorologist likes to be called a weatherman. One is a scientist, the other an actor.

"Yeah, right," he says laughing.

"At least until the next models come in," I say tossing the pillow at him. "Just keep me informed."

"I will darlin'. But seriously, try to relax about it. It will be a few more days before I can give you a solid forecast."

Relax is not a word in my vocabulary this week. In addition to a flurry of final details for the race, I am just flat out stoked about the fact that it is finally here.

"Hey, did I tell you that Channel 4 asked me to be on their air this week?"

"What?"

"Yeah, they want me to be on their morning show on Friday. Sam Kouvaris has apparently been wearing our running ribbon tie and talking up the race all last week. Is that sweet or what?"

"Donna, that is awesome!"

This is almost unheard of in local television. A competing station willing to pump an event connected to another station's anchor. It was my fondest hope when I started planning all this that the cause and the scope of the race would transcend all of that. This is truly a milestone.

"So you go on their air Friday morning?"

"Well it depends on the station. I have to get permission."

"Well, surely they'll let you do it."

"I take nothing for granted."

The phone rings. It's Julie Terrazzano, director of the Donna Foundation.

"Hey, Jules, what's up?"

"I just wanted to let you know that I have Debra Sullins set up for your crew to interview this week. She's a DF recipient and really a perfect example of the women we serve. Her husband lost his job the day she was diagnosed. Can you believe that? She has small children and she's just finished her chemo. She volunteered to tell her story. We helped her with her mortgage and other critical needs throughout her treatment. She is anxious to let everyone know how the Foundation helped her get through it all."

"Great. People need to know what we're about. You know I don't like to ask recipients to talk, but since she volunteered I feel good about it."

Since the Foundation started nearly five years ago, we have helped more than 1500 women like Debra. We pay their mortgages, child care, car payments, medications. Whatever they need to get through until they can get back on their feet. I remember so vividly a conversation I had with one of our first recipients.

"You make the choice for me, Donna. I can put food on the table for my kids or buy my meds."

No choice at all.

"So how are you holding up this week?" Julie asks.

"I'm a freaked out ball of stress, but besides that, fine."

"It's going to be great, Donna. How are you feeling, physically?"

I look down at my hands and feet. They are beet red, swollen, and peeling. My hands feel like the visual of one of those cartoon characters who hits his hand with a hammer. The result is a throbbing hand three times its size. I can barely put weight on my feet. Feels like I've been walking on hot coals.

"My hands and feet are a mess. But I'm not going to think about it."

"Are you still going to run?"

"Of course I'm going to run. Just haven't decided whether to do the full or the half."

"You're crazy. Do you know that? Hey, speaking of crazy. My brother Craig just called and said he heard a rumor that Oprah Winfrey is running the marathon. Is that true?"

"God, I wish! How do these things get started? No, I'm afraid that one is just a rumor."

"Maybe we should spread it."

"Good idea. I also heard a rumor that today is your birthday."

"You have to remind me."

"Of course I have to remind you that you are still, and always will be, older than me."

"By two weeks."

"Two and a half."

"I'll talk to you later," she says laughing.

"See you, old woman."

I hang up the phone and immediately dial Jason Raphael. He is the First Coast News producer in charge of race week coverage. We go through the list of possible stories.

"We'll need to interview Sgt. Leonard Propper on road closures and Theresa Price about the race day shuttles."

"Got it."

"Also, Scott Silvers and some other Mayo docs are doing something pretty cool. They are doing research on runners who agree to be tested both before and after the race. They'll sign up anyone who is interested at the expo. They'll take blood samples, temperature, blood pressure, weight, and so on. Then after they cross the finish line the runners will go to the medical tent and they'll get the same readings. The idea is to see how the body responds to the stress of an endurance event. They're calling it Runner's Science. This year will be the beginning of a multi-year study."

Tap, tap tap. I can hear Jason's fingers flying across his computer keyboard as we speak.

"I like that. Runner's Science," he repeats as he types. "We should probably also go over the types of breast cancer research Dr. Perez is hoping to do with the race dollars."

"Yes, I want people to understand exactly where their money is going. Oh, and we will definitely want to do something with Joan Benoit Samuelson. She's our rock star runner, but she won't be here until the expo."

I still can't believe my running hero is going to be at the race. Samuelson is an icon in women's running. She was the winner of the first ever Women's Olympic Marathon event in Los Angeles in 1984 and she is still setting records for her age group. She's one of those amazing athletes who just seem to get stronger with age. Joanie, as everyone calls her, will be running our half marathon as the final race before she competes in the Olympic trials at the Boston Marathon in April. She is 50 years old and her goal is to run a 2:50 at 50. A 2:50 marathon. That's a sub 6:30 pace. The thought of it boggles my mind. My best marathon ever was barely sub four hours. I can't even fathom speed like that.

My friend Keith Brantly, an Olympic marathoner himself in 1996 and the 1998 U.S. marathon champion, is responsible for getting Samuelson to agree to come to our race. They are old friends and Keith graciously accepted my request to be in charge of our elite athletes. Those are the professionals who will compete for the prize money. They'll be crossing the finish line before many of the runners have made it half way through the course.

"Joan Benoit Samuelson. She's on my list. Donna, can you hang on a minute."

"Sure."

"Can someone please turn down that scanner? I can't even hear myself think here," he shouts into the newsroom.

I can tell he has tried to cover the mouthpiece with his hand but his voice is so loud I momentarily pull the phone away from my ear.

"Sorry," he says, returning to the conversation. "Sometimes I want to take a hammer to that police scanner."

"There might be some money in it for you," I say. "I've got a hammer in my kitchen drawer."

"Don't tempt me. OK, I'm assuming you want to be live at the expo on Friday."

"Absolutely. All shows. I'd like to be right outside the expo hall."

"As long as the weather cooperates that should be fine. What's Tim saying about that?"

"Friday looks perfect."

"And Sunday?"

"Iffy."

15 | *My* Sunny Valentine

February 14, 2008

"Give me one reason I shouldn't quit!" I say, while sopping up coffee I've just spilled all over the kitchen counter.

"I'll give you a stack of them," Tim says. "Just take a look in there."

He points to the drawer next to the fridge where we keep all of our bills.

"The last time I checked we still had a mortgage, and we have kids to get through college."

He is right, of course. I am just bitterly disappointed. The managers at the station have just turned down my request for the race interview with our rival station.

I reach for another paper towel, and shove it around the tan stone surface like sandpaper.

"I begged, you know. I practically begged them. It is so important to me that this race become a national event, one that everyone wants to cover. That starts right here in Jacksonville. That's the only way we raise enough money to make a huge difference. I'm not just giving lip service to ending this disease, Tim. I want it finished. And do they think my mission for the underserved is just some sideshow for me? This is life. It shouldn't be about competition. Besides, it only makes them look good to support it. Why don't they get it?"

I slam dunk the pile of coffee soaked paper towels into the trash and look to Tim for an answer.

"I don't know. It makes no sense. I guess they just can't see the big picture. What reason did they give you?"

"They just said they didn't want to promote the competition. Hello? I am the First Coast News Anchor. Even if they can't take the high road for philanthropy, you'd think at least they'd see the advantages of having their anchor on the competition's air. It's a free ad, for heaven's sake," I say, throwing my arms in the air.

"I totally agree. It's a shame, but you have to look on the positive side."

I stare at Tim, incredulous.

"Yeah, what's that?"

"It shows how much they value you."

"Excuse me?"

"Think about it, Donna. If they didn't think you were important to their success they wouldn't consider it a threat to have you on the other station. I know it's flawed reasoning, but at least they aren't apathetic about you."

My husband is the least judgmental man on earth. No matter what the situation, he finds a way to look at things from the other person's perspective. He assumes everyone is coming from a good place. I love this about him even if I can't always see the same light in the darkness.

"You are beyond belief," I say shaking my head. But I am reminded, as I am a hundred times a day, why this man is so good for me.

I lean over and kiss Tim on the cheek. "I'm glad you're my Valentine even if you won't take the low road with me," I say.

Tim starts to defend himself but I raise a finger to his lips.

"No need to apologize for being who you are, my love."

I move my finger and plant a kiss in the same spot.

"Thank you, Mi Amore," he says fixing me in his deep blue gaze.

"I have a Valentine's present for you," he says.

"Peterbrooke chocolate popcorn, I hope."

"That's for later. Check your computer. Just sent you an updated forecast for Sunday. We still have to watch it, but the models seem to be converging around the idea that the front won't come through until well after the race is over, either late Sunday night or Monday morning."

"Better than chocolate," I say.

We are only three days out now and the closer we get, the more reliable the forecast becomes.

I click in to Tim's email.

Here is the 2/14 Update

FRIDAY: SUNNY - P/C WINDS NE 5 LO/HI 40-67

SATURDAY: SUNNY — P/C WINDS NE 10 LO/HI 50-66

SUNDAY: 6:30AM -3:30 SUNNY — P/C WINDS SE 15 LO/HI 58-72

T-STORMS HOLD OFF UNTIL AFTER 9PM!

HAPPY VALENTINES DAY

The rain is still a little close for my comfort and I'm keeping an eye on the heat. Everyone is paranoid since the Chicago marathon was cut short due to extreme heat last October, but those temperatures were far warmer than any predicted for us. I say a little prayer for Susan to come through and forward the forecast to the rest of my team, plus my family and friends.

Among the runners who, according to the registration stats, now hail from every state and 15 countries, will be a handful of my relatives from Greenville, South Carolina. I'm having the entire clan including Tim's family over for brunch on Saturday. Tim's sister Mary Pat is coming in from Minnesota with her son David. Mary Pat and Tim's mom Margie are volunteering at the race expo that opens tomorrow. That's where all the runners will pick up their race packets, pasta load, and hopefully do plenty of shopping before the race on Sunday.

My sister Tara, my aunts Evelyn and Mary and Mary's daughter Lindsay are all doing the half marathon. My mother, just coming off her back surgery, will have to be content to watch.

"I'm doing the half marathon next year," she told me, her tone daring me to tell her otherwise. My mother is 70. She thinks she can still do everything she did when she was 30. Love the attitude. Hate the medical bills.

Mom's youngest brother, David, my senior by about 17 months, is still trying to decide whether he will do the half or the full. David and I have been trading emails for weeks on this topic. He started off training for the full, but fractured his foot and had to take some time off. He did get his miles up to 18 before he had to stop, so that should give him some confidence. I see his name on my list of new messages. We're two days from the race and like me he is still on the fence.

From: David G. Barnett

Sent: February 14, 2008

Subject: I'm Nervous

I know what I should do....run the half....but I know what I want to do....run the full. I haven't run longer than 14 miles in two months.

You have done this before....do you honestly think I can run the full?
I just can't quite imagine what 26.2 would feel like. I probably
will do what you do. Seriously...can I do it and what and when was
your last long run?

I write back some words of encouragement.

I haven't run more than 13 since September but I do know I could
do it.

I just don't know if I SHOULD do it! I will be proud of you no
matter what. You absolutely can do it if you want to. It's all
mental.

I think you said you got in 18. That's plenty. It would have been
nice for time purposes had you gotten in a couple more, but for
distance you are definitely cool. I am just not a good spectator.

I want to play. Also, I'm afraid I will be mad at myself if I am
not out there experiencing the whole thing. That said, I still
won't know until Sunday. Wish I could be more helpful.

Do what feels right to you. Prepare like you are going to run the
full.

Hydrate and carbo load (the fun part) and just see where the
moment takes you.

It's going to be great!

I let myself drift once more to race day. I really want to run the full marathon. Is it foolish? Jeff thinks it's not such a hot idea for my immune system. And what about my feet?

Just follow your own advice, Donna. Get up on race day and let the moment decide for you.

A few of the anchors and reporters at First Coast News, led by my colleagues Phil Amato, Patty Crosby and Deanna Fené, are planning to run a relay to complete the second half of the marathon if I can run 13. They'll be waiting for me at the Jacksonville Beach Pier. That's the turnaround point for the half marathon.

OK, so I have until then to make my decision. I can run the first 6 and a half and see how I feel.

My Boston buddy Nancy Bauer, another breast cancer survivor whom I affectionately call "my pahd-nah in crime", is flying down to run with me and Tim. She is planning to run the Boston Marathon in two months in memory of her sister Suzanne so she has already informed me that she won't be going the whole distance. Nancy and I have been pals since the year I ran Boston as a fundraiser for Dana Farber. We've been through many runs and several breast cancer recurrences together. She calls her offending breast "the evil twin".

"We're just running the half, right?" This has become my question from Nancy at least three times a week since she decided to make the trip.

"That's the plan. I haven't run more than 13 miles so the likelihood that I would run the whole thing is very small," I tell her.

She knows me too well.

"OK, well I'm just telling you, if you get a wild hair and decide to run the full marathon, I'm not coming with you. I'm out after the half, pahd-nah. You got it? I've had a wicked sore hamstring for a few weeks and I'm not going to aggravate it."

I know her too well.

"Uh huh, I'm fine with that Nancy. Just make sure you pack your Motrin."

"I'm not kidding," she says.

"I know."

We go back and forth like this in every conversation. Nancy is one of the toughest and most loyal people I know. Over the years we've often gone for months without talking, but we know each other's hearts so completely, we can always just pick up wherever we left off.

Tim's voice brings me back to the present.

"I'm headed west," he says.

That's Tim's way of saying he's going to work.

"OK, sweetheart, I'll see you in there," I say as we share a quick kiss.

"Tell the boss I'll be there right after I drop off my job application at Channel 4."

Tim sighs.

"Kidding," I say, flashing an exaggerated smile.

"Remember the paycheck darlin'," he says, returning the grin. "Besides, I sent your chocolate to the office."

16 | Gift Wrap

February 15, 2008

Still three blocks away from the expo and already I can see the sign. It's huge.

I pull into the parking lot of the Morocco Shrine Auditorium and don't even recognize the place. When Theresa first suggested this location for the expo I was less than thrilled. The building is old and outdated. Hardly the impression I wanted to leave for our first race.

"Don't worry," she told me. "You know how they wrap cars these days? Well we are just going the wrap the building."

"Right, you are going the wrap an entire building."

"Yes. Given the price they are giving us versus the others, we can literally make over the building for less money than it would cost to rent space in a big hotel."

I was skeptical to say the least. But what I'm looking at now is exactly what Theresa with all her amazing vision described. She has literally wrapped the Morocco Shrine Auditorium Sign with one that says 26.2 With Donna. It looks like the whole place belongs to us. Our running ribbon logo must be 20 feet tall.

The columns leading up to the building are all wrapped in our logo as well. The walkway to the expo hall is covered in bright pink carpet. A huge map of the course sits out front next to a logoed screen for people who want to take pictures. Balloons are everywhere and volunteers stand at the entrance with pink shopping bags ready to hand them to everyone who enters. Every inch of the place is decked out. I stand at the opening to the expo hall in stunned silence.

"Like it?"

There beside me is Barry Rabinowitz, a local photographer who has been hired by *Runner's World* magazine to shoot pictures of the race. He'll be going up in a helicopter Sunday morning to get "the money shot". When thousands of us stream over the J. Turner Butler Bridge toward the ocean, Barry will capture the long ribbon of runners against the beauty of the intracoastal marsh. It's a picture I've painted in my mind a million times. I can't wait to see it for real.

"Like it? It's unbelievable," I say.

"Mind if I follow you around for a while? I'd like to get some reaction shots."

In truth, I sort of do mind. I fell asleep working on race mail last night and I never even took off my makeup. After a few hours sleep I threw on some clothes, put my hair in a pony tail and raced down here to see the expo before it opens. My mascara is smudged, my blush is uneven. I basically look like a drag queen.

"Sure, Barry," I say. "Just not too close on the close-ups OK?"

Walking from booth to booth I watch the vendors setting up their stations. There is a huge Mayo Clinic booth at the entrance, and one for the Donna Foundation. All of our official marathon gear is laid out in its own store. Then further down, there are booths for all of our sponsors, Sanofi Aventis, Genentech, Bristol Myers Squibb, Glaxo Smith- Kline, Amgen. Everyone is working diligently to set up before the doors open.

I spot the woman with iRUNLIKEAGIRL, one of the only major national vendors we've been able to hook for our inaugural.

"Thank you so much for coming," I say.

"Hey, a race that's 75 percent women for a cause. This is going to be a shopfest. And I'm so impressed with the organization. I just hope I brought enough merchandise."

We chat for a few minutes.

"I appreciate the support," I say sincerely, moving on to the packet pick up area.

There I thank the volunteers who are preparing for what will no doubt be a hectic couple of days. There are actually two-thousand volunteers who will be working the race between the expo and the marathon. It's a big time commitment with a lot of homework involved. They need to be able to answer any question that comes their way and there will be some weird ones.

"You all are so awesome to help us with all this," I say to a group setting up a table of finisher shirts. "Are you ready for the crowds?"

"We're ready," says one woman, her eyes sparkling with excitement. Nods and thumbs up from the rest.

In the far back end of the expo a giant screen shows scenes from our training runs, stories about Edith and the success she has seen in breast cancer research at Mayo, and testimonials from women who have benefitted from the Donna Foundation. Beside the screen a pink life guard chair and a beach umbrella set the scene for our coastal theme.

This is genius.

I make my way up the center aisle with Barry in tow. There, stretched across a long table, is an enormous banner where the runners will write the names of those they want to honor and remember. There are already a few scattered names and quotes from the volunteers who are working the expo. I grab a marker and step up to the banner. Begin writing first Susan's name, then Laurie's. One after another the names of so many women come into my head. As I write tears pour down my face along with the remaining mascara. Barry is right beside me, and now so is our expo coordinator, Jane Alred.

Jane and her husband Doug are the owners of First Place Sports, a local running store. They are the organizers for practically every race in Jacksonville including the nation's largest 15k, The Gate River Run. My team will be running that race next month. Doug has played a large role in getting the course ready for Sunday and will time the event for us.

"I thought you'd love it," says Jane wrapping her arm around my shoulder.

"I wasn't prepared," I say, choking on my tears.

"Jane this whole place is just beyond belief."

"I think we are going to have a huge crowd, too. I'm getting so many calls from people wanting to make sure they can sign up at the expo."

In future years I hope we are large enough to close registration early. That would make these final days less chaotic and make planning easier all the way around. For now though, we just want as many runners as we can get.

"Great, are you ready?"

"Of course. Have you seen Kurtis' booth yet?"

"No, not yet."

"Well, if the banners got you, you may want to grab some tissues before you head down there."

"I'm sure I am quite the sight."

"You look great. Let yourself have some fun today. We're all set here."

Kurtis' booth is the highlight of the entire expo. He has all of his artwork from our training sessions matted and some of it framed. He has our inaugural poster, a sea of pink runners on the beach, with the bridge and the lifeguard station in the background, and behind him, he's created walls made from runner's images and excerpts from our Why I'm Running stories from the website. I want to soak in every word.

Why I'm Running

My friend Steve lost his wife, I lost my Mother and Sister both died from cancer . . . I will help anyone who needs someone to run with in the Atlanta area to get in shape . . . we are running to help the fight on cancer.

Charles Dorman–Marietta, Ga.

>>>>

This is such a great blessing for us, yet I want to support in any way possible, those women that have suffered from this disease. I run for them, their courage, strength and beauty. I run for our family's blessing.

Debra Davey–Jacksonville, FL

>>>>

My friend Karin died in 2007 of inflammatory breast cancer, after fighting it for 5 long years. It's just a crime against nature that her two kids should have to grow up without her loving influence in their lives, and I want to do what I can to prevent other children from going through such a rough time. Karin was one of the most beautiful spirits I have ever known, and my life is much less bright without her in it.

Amy Hoover

>>>>

My mom and my Aunt are survivors. This is my way of giving back. This is my way to help someone whom I have never met. This is my way to show other that I care. 13.1 miles -- 26.2 miles -- as a runner or walker is hard -- but can be done. As our team in training motto goes -- If you think training for a marathon is hard, try CHEMO! I have been graced in my life to have many wonderful people in my life. On February 17th this one is for you mom!

Pamela Matherne–New Orleans

>>>>

My mom runs marathons, even after her double mastectomy last year. Just 3 weeks after her surgery, she walked 5 miles in the Susan G. Komen run/walk. She is an incredible strong woman; she and I are running together. She thinks this will be her 48th marathon; it will be my first.

I am running for/with my mom. I am running for my boss who survived stage 4 breast cancer; I am running for my friend who didn't. I will run for those who are strong incredible women who have fought and are fighting breast cancer.

Tommiann Hill–Greensboro, NC

>>>>

My beautiful mother passed away just one year ago from breast cancer. She was only 49. She raised 5 of us virtually by herself. She watched three of her sons who were Marines enter and leave Iraq several times. She lost everything she ever owned in Katrina and then she lost her battle with breast cancer right when she should have been starting her life over again. I will run in her memory and to try to fight this disease which I have come to hate. I want to run this marathon so that maybe one day no one will have to face this sorrow.

Lisa Berger–South Carolina

>>>>

I met a wonderful woman when I was 14 years old. She held my hand as I recovered from my first Breast Biopsy when I was 15. She saw me grow into a woman and I eventually married her son. A beautiful woman with so much life. She laughed easily and lived humbly. She went to church and sang in choir. This woman, my mother-in-law, Linda Toussaint , was diagnosed with Breast Cancer in 1992.

She became a survivor. In 2003 she was diagnosed a second time.

Although, knowing the chances for a second time diagnosis, she under went treatment and was present later that year when my son was born. On January 3, 2005, I held my mother-in-law's hand as the doctor explained that the cancer had returned and that this time it was not treatable. She passed away November 2005 at the age of 54. This is why I run. I run in the memory of Linda Toussaint. I run to help fight the good fight.

Penny Punnett–Jacksonville, Florida

>>>>

I am a two year breast cancer survivor I began running after I ended all my treatments as a way to begin living a healthier life and fight back against this disease that had entered my life. I am so excited to be coming to this event with my wonderful husband (and greatest caregiver in the world), a dear friend who was with me during treatments, and a sister-in-law who has supported me through these past two years with love and encouragement. I hope to encourage others to fight back against this disease and not let it take away their spirit and hope.

Belinda Johnson

>>>>

Last August 2006, before a major running race, I was diagnosed with a life threatening condition and was hospitalized. I was not able to run for several months and when I did I started back with a new enthusiasm knowing that I got a second chance in life. Now, I want to help give a second chance to women living with breast cancer. Running for my life.

Eva Sanmartini–Flint, Michigan

>>>>

I share a common thread that weaves the fabric of your marathon. I too am a breast cancer survivor and a runner. On top of my breast cancer diagnosis, I was diagnosed with Multiple Sclerosis. On a very physically and emotionally challenging day, I opened my new issue of Runner's World to the page advertising "26.2 with Donna" (great name by the way . . .). There looking back at me was my newest goal. From that moment I made a commitment to run with you. A perfect opportunity for me to do what I do best . . . run. I have been running for nearly 30 years (yikes!). Running has been part of my life, recovery, and renewal for a very long time. So after a lengthy forced hiatus, I am back! I will continue to run, staying ahead of breast cancer and MS. Neither will catch me! So, here's to all of us who have survived and live each day and for those who fought the battle and sadly lost the war. Thank you for taking on this worthy endeavor! I plan to raise lots of money for the cause. Let's Go!! See you there!

Donna Davis- Rankin–Manchester, Maine

>>>>

My precious wife lived with cancer for six years. After two different primary tumors three years apart and then numerous recurrences, she finally won the final victory on April 23, 2007 when she was called home to heaven. My Marla leaves behind two boys, nearly 6 and 10, who desperately long for their momma to tuck them in at night and a husband is mourning her moment by moment. We don't want anyone else to have to journey where we are. Together, let's keep fighting and running to end this disease and all of its pain.

Steve Quinn–Sugar Hill, GA

>>>>

When I was 7 my grandmother, the foundation and core of who I am, was taken away from me at the age of 59 after a long drawn out battle with breast cancer. Her fight was lost 17 years ago, and not a day goes by that I don't think about her. I became a runner in Junior High and continued on through college. I have never run a marathon and am excited to run my first one in memory of my grandmother. I have great respect for any survivor and consider it a great honor to run next to many of them.

Good luck to all.

Kelly Ryan

> > > >

Kurtis has his back to me, setting up an easel.

He looks up to see me standing there with my mouth wide open.

"Well, say something," he finally says, his eyes already wet with emotion.

I can't. I just walk over and pull him into an embrace and we are both crying.

This is personal. We have all worked so hard. Our vision has been so clear. We all sense the enormity of what's happening. The potential for good. The lives we can touch. The difference we can all make. The movies we have been playing in our minds are materializing right before our eyes and the emotions at seeing it all come together are simply too much to hold back.

My intention to spend a few minutes before the opening turns into hours. I have no desire to leave. I go to the bathroom, wash my face and begin to greet the thousands of people who will be among the difference makers this weekend.

Back at home, I type out an email to Theresa and her right hand Sarah Horn.

From: Donna Deegan

Sent: Friday, February 15, 2008 1:10 PM

To: Price, Theresa; Horn, Sarah

Subject: I have no words

To adequately tell either one of you how blown away I am at the expo. I have been crying for hours.

Thank you so much.

And Sarah when I saw the banner I just lost it. Wow!

The nicest compliment came from the woman at Runs Like a Girl. She said the big vendors usually never come to first time events but she saw how first class everything seemed and decided to come anyway. She said in all her time at expos she has never seen one so well done. She was so impressed by the way you dressed the building. So impressed by everything.

She's afraid she won't have enough stuff and is sad everyone else really missed out but would definitely be here next year.

Good stuff.

I hit send and burrow into more race mail. From the very beginning I have insisted on answering all of it myself. I want to personally connect with everyone who writes in about the race. This worked beautifully at first when the emails came in a few at a time. For the past several weeks, though, dozens are coming in each day and I'm having a tough time keeping up. Also, the early correspondences were mostly just letters of excitement and congratulations from runners saying "hey it's about time we had a marathon for breast cancer!" Lots of pats on the back, some stories and a few questions. Now during the week of the race, most of the people who email have an issue that I need to resolve. The first one makes me laugh.

The National Marathon to Fight Breast Cancer – Contact Form

Subject: Race Number

Message: I picked up my race number today and it lists me as a

50 yo man, when I am actually a 50 yo woman. On the envelope it is correct but on the number it is wrong. I would really like this corrected before the race. Please contact me regarding this asap.

Subject: Race Confirmation

Message:I lost my race confirmation card to pick up my number on Sunday. How can I pick up my number without having the card? Can I bring my print version of my registration confirmation?

Subject: Contribution

Message:The other day I made a contribution for JP Buchanan's race in memory of his wife, Paula, in the amount of $25.00. I don't think I went to the right site. Is there any way you could make sure this donation shows up on his site. Thank you.

Subject: Packet pick up

Message:I am unable to pick up my race packet because I cannot get off the island I live on in the Bahamas until 6:30 tomorrow evening. Can I please pick up my packet on race day. I can meet anyone at the start. I will be there right after 5:00 in the morning. I will be staying at the Best Western on 4660 Salisbury Rd Jacksonville, FL. I will take the bus at the Best Western where I am staying at Saturday night. Please help me.

Subject: pre-race

Message:Since we HAVE to use shuttles, arriving at the latest,

1 hour before start, temps are going to be about 50 deg, I have no one

to hand stuff off to before the race - how exactly are we going to be

able to stay warm? Would love to have someone with, but they'd never

just stand around for 3 hours waiting for me to come back. This is

going to be the worst part of the whole race . . . ugh. sorry . . . .original

plan was someone to drop me off, go home, come back later, you know?

Subject: Getting out

Message:I live on Saturiba Dr and have to leave at 1:30 pm to

get to a wedding will I be able to leave?

Subject: Confirmation Card

Message:This is to confirm that Maryane Dinkins will be

retreiving the 1/2 marathon packet in my name, Robertyo Tejada, insofar

as I will be arriving late to JAX from California.

The issue of race packet pick up is a sticky one. Race packets must be picked up at the expo. It's just too crazy on race morning to be handing out packets, yet dozens of people are coming out of the woodwork at the last second with reasons why they can't do this. I dial Theresa. To my relief, she picks up immediately.

"Hey lady, I hear you like your expo?"

"Oh my gosh Theresa, did you get my email? That's the understatement of the world. You and Sarah and your whole team, you are all miracle workers! I could go on and on about it all day, but I have some problems with packet pick up I need to discuss with you."

We go over it for the umpteenth time. Everyone thinks their problem is the only one. And if that were true, it would be easy enough to hand out one packet on race morning. But with police, and volunteers and medical personnel, and runners to corral, it's just too much. But I want to make sure we are doing the right thing.

"OK, so I tell everyone they have to either have someone pick up their packet at the expo or they can't run. It's just the only way to be fair to everyone."

"Good," Theresa says. "Hey does that cute husband of yours have an updated forecast for me today?"

"It looks mostly the same. I'm going to have him send out a final version tomorrow. You have enough water for me, right?"

"Donna, I have enough water to fill the St. Johns River. Relax about the water. The Mayo folks are anticipating a warm day as are our EMTs so we're good. Will you just have some fun today? Everything is covered."

This is the second time today someone has suggested I have fun. The truth is as frenetic as everything is I am having more fun than I have ever had in my life.

17 | $\mathcal{M}$y Inner Kenyan

February 16, 2008

"We have two minutes, Donna."

Photographer Josh Sanchez gives me the cue that we are getting close to our live report.

"OK, we need to find Lorraine and Dan Hardaway. They are going to be my first interviews."

"They're coming," he says.

Standing inside the pre-race pasta party. The six o'clock newscast has just begun.

Lorraine and Dan bound up next to me, their faces radiant with excitement. Dan was the winner of our free trip to Jacksonville for the race. At every race expo we've attended around the country, from New York to L.A. we have given folks a chance to sign up. The winner gets an all expense paid trip to the marathon, and entrance to the race at no cost. Our winners happen to be from Orlando. They signed up at the Disney Marathon expo, and it turns out they are already huge supporters of the race.

"Standby, Donna," Josh says.

I nod. Then, through my IFB, the earpiece through which I hear the anchors and producers talking to me, comes the voice of our weekend anchor Victor Blackwell.

"At last count, 7000 runners are in Jacksonville tonight for the inaugural running of 26.2 With Donna The National Marathon to Fight Breast Cancer, and First Coast News Anchor Donna Deegan joins us live from the what I consider the fun part, the pre-race pasta load. Donna registration has just gone through the roof today.

"Victor, we have had more than a thousand people sign up just at the expo alone. We had expected about 5000 for our inaugural, so this crowd has really surpassed our expectations. And yes, while we think of the whole event as the fun part, you're right carbo-loading is a lot of fun."

Josh zooms out to show my guests standing next to me.

"Here, enjoying the pasta party with me, are Dan and Lorraine Hardaway. Dan won our drawing for a free trip to the race but Dan we found out you were already signed up to run."

"Yes Donna, Lorraine and I run with a group from the Track Shack in Orlando. We have a special runner who is an inspiration to all of us, her name is also Donna. We are supporting her through her fight with breast cancer and we're really excited to be here."

"And Lorraine, you two have been our ambassadors down in central Florida. You've brought a bunch of people up with you."

"Yes we have! We have a great group at the Track Shack and we are going to continue to support you and this race. It's great to finally have a marathon distance race just dedicated to the cause of breast cancer. We are already so impressed with everything. Our Donna is here too. She won't be running this year because of her chemo, but we'll be running for her."

"I know I speak for your Donna and all the others survivors out there when I say we are truly grateful for that. Lorraine, Dan, we couldn't have asked for nicer people to win our trip. Thank you for your support and have a great run out there tomorrow."

"Thanks Donna, we'll see you out there, right?"

"Yes, you will."

I turn back to the camera and address Victor.

"Victor, in the next few minutes we will be talking with the first women's Olympic Marathon champion, Joan Benoit Samuelson. For now, I'm going to load up on some pasta."

"So Donna, before you go, I heard you tell Lorraine that you'll be running tomorrow. Everyone wants to know have you decided on the full marathon or the half?"

"I'll know tomorrow, Victor. I really haven't made a decision."

"OK, we'll wait and see. In the meantime, we'll check back in with you in a few minutes. Enjoy the pasta."

I put down the microphone and am startled to see Joanie at my shoulder. I still can't believe Joan Benoit Samuelson is here at my race. What a kick!

"Joanie, thank you again for being here. It just makes everything perfect. When would you like to speak with the crowd?"

"Any time you're ready. Did I hear you say you are thinking about running the full marathon?"

"I'm thinking about it."

A look of concern covers her face.

"Don't do that. Just run the half. Why would you want to tax your body like that in the middle of your chemo?"

"I'll only run if I'm feeling good. We'll see."

"Listen, if you just run the half, I'll come out and run you in," she persists.

This is tempting. I could be running with Joanie Benoit. I let my mind create the scene. Donna and Joanie, striding together across the finish line.

"Well, you might have to slow down just a wee bit," I say holding my thumb and forefinger about a half inch apart.

I turn to Josh.

"How long before we go live again?"

"About 7 minutes."

"OK, Joanie, if you'd like to welcome the crowd, I think you have time. I'd like to interview you live after that."

"Sounds great."

Joanie works her magic with the crowd and after our live broadcast I take a load off my feet for what seems like the first time today. I load a plate with pasta and sit down beside her and our mutual friend Keith Brantly.

"Have you rested at all through all of this?" she asks.

"Oh gosh, I don't guess I have. I just feel like I need to be everywhere. I want to be everywhere. I can't tell you how much fun I'm having soaking it all in."

"I'll bet. And wouldn't it be nice to just run the half tomorrow and be there to greet all those marathoners coming in. You could personally put a medal around their necks. That would be very special."

"I hear you, Joanie. I just think it would also be special for people, especially survivors, to see that I am out there doing the whole race. I want people to know they can do it too. I'm not saying I'm going to do the whole thing, I just don't know."

"Do what feels right to you Donna," Keith says. "I love your shirt."

It's been such a long day, I have to double check to see what I'm wearing.

In My Mind I'm A Kenyan

The words are written in bold dark green letters across my bright pink shirt. I bought it at the Mon-Tees booth at the expo yesterday.

"I'm wearing this to remind myself that 99 percent of what I will do out there on the course tomorrow is in my mind, not in my red swollen feet," I say.

"You've got that right," Keith says.

Sufficiently pasta loaded, we say our goodnights and go home.

Tim immediately looks at the latest weather maps and types out his final pre-race forecast. I read it and forward the verdict to our entire team.

From: Donna Deegan

Date: Sat, 16 Feb 2008

Folks we couldn't have asked for a more perfect lead up. Thank you to all!

Here is your final weather update from Tim as of 9:30pm.

I am so proud of all of you!

Here's to a great day tomorrow!

6am – 57 Degrees Winds Southeast at 5mph

8:30 -59 Degrees Winds Southeast at 5mph Sunny to Partly Cloudy

Noon- 72 Degrees Winds Southeast at 15mph

3:30 – 71 Degrees Southeast at 15 to 20

20 percent chance of showers after 8pm

Strong T-storms early MONDAY morning

Although certainly we want to prepare for the heat, let's keep this in perspective.

Chicago went 67 to 87. Dew point rose to the lower 70's.

Our dew point will not get over 62.

My first response back is from Theresa Price. Short and sweet.

We are ready for whatever the weather throws our way . . . .

Good luck to all!

T.

The last before I log off, comes from Keith.

Donna! Now it's time for you to take care of you! Focus on your race, imagine yourself floating, not running each step. Your stride is smoother, longer and more beautiful than any Kenyan! In my mind, I am Donna!

WE LOVE YOU!

You go girl!

Keith

18 | Pink Ribbon in the Sky

February 17, 2008

Tim and I turn onto San Pablo road just after 6 a.m. We are less than two and a half hours to race time and the butterflies in my stomach feel more like Pterodactyls. My half eaten banana is sitting on the counter at home and my coffee is getting cold in the cup holder of Tim's car.

Usually I'm meticulous about how I eat the morning before a race. We all have our little rituals. Mine is dry toast, half a cup of yogurt, and a banana, a few hours before the start. Today I was lucky to down two bites of the banana and my gut said thanks, but no thanks.

Tim is like a kid at Christmas. I am wound tight as a drum.

"Relax darlin'. All the work is done now," he says squeezing my leg. "It's time to just enjoy your day."

I give him a small nervous smile. I am literally shaking.

As we approach the entrance to the Mayo Clinic, which is also the start/finish line, Tim rolls down his window to speak with the police officer in charge of traffic flow there. It is still pitch black outside. We are at the access for the command center and, at first, the officer tries to wave us on. Then there's a look of recognition and his face breaks into a smile.

"Good morning Deegans! Right this way," he says.

"Thanks for being out here," Tim says and we roll on.

The officer calls on his radio to the next check point and we are waved all the way through to the parking lot where Theresa and her team are already humming along with great precision.

We park the car and Tim takes my hand.

"I'm very proud of you," he says, looking into my eyes.

"Thank you, my love," I say pulling his hand to my lips.

"Let yourself breathe, Donna."

I take a deep breath and do my best to settle into the moment. The minutes right before any marathon are emotional, but this race has been the child I've been carrying for two years. Now that it is about to come into the world, I'm just overwhelmed. The chemo sort of puts that into overdrive. I always tell people being on chemo is like PMS on speed.

"Want to go check out the Runner's Village?" Tim asks.

"Let's say hello to the folks at the medical tent and check in with Theresa on our way over," I say.

The medical tent is just at the end of the parking lot and I can see doctors, nurses and volunteers working steadily to set up.

"How is everyone this morning?" I ask walking into the tent.

"Ready to go," says a tall auburn haired woman. She's wearing a shirt with a red cross indicating a member of the Mayo medical staff. "Tim, it looks like a warm one."

"Yes, it's going to be warm. Shouldn't go over about 72 but for runners that's going to cause some stress. Hopefully the sea breeze will kick in early and we'll get at least some relief."

"We are anticipating some heat reactions, but everyone's excited to be here. This is really something, isn't it?"

"It certainly is," Tim says.

"Thanks everybody. Good luck today," I say.

We continue on to the command center where Theresa has a phone to her ear, a person talking to her, another waiting to talk, and a police radio blasting instructions on a table next to her. I wait until I can get in a word edgewise.

"Hey there Super Woman," I say. "You got everybody in line this morning?"

She is in the Theresa Zone. I love this.

"Everything is going along as planned. The shuttles started leaving the hotels about an hour ago. Joe Trottie tells me that's going very smoothly. Leonard has his men at all the intersections along the course. Luann and the Mayo medical team are setting up. Deb's volunteers have been here working most of the night.

She looks down at her notepad.

"Water's all dropped at the water and aid stations, GU's there, Doug Alred is about to start race announcements and then Jeff Galloway will officially welcome the crowd. Do you have the list of sponsors you need to thank?

"I don't have a list of anything."

She turns to Sarah.

"Sarah, do you have Donna's remarks?"

Sarah hands me several sheets of paper, neatly organized and numbered.

"This is your sponsor thank you list. The rest is just a schedule of the announcements you need to make," Sarah says.

"What time?"

She looks at Theresa.

"Oh I'd say Doug and Jeff have it handled until about a half hour before race time. But you may want to head that way early. I hear you have 7000 of your closest friends coming and you tend to be friendly," she says.

"Can you believe this day is finally here, T?"

"Yes, I told you when you came to me two years ago that everything is possible. You just have to believe. Money doesn't hurt either."

"Amen to that sister."

We have been incredibly fortunate to have many generous sponsors. They've made it possible for us to send all the money we raise from the race to our chosen charities. Unlike most charity groups who ask their runners to raise a set amount of cash to participate, we make fundraising voluntary. A runner's entrance fee is all that is needed. Many people have chosen to fundraise. And now those dollars alone are over the $400,000 mark.

"I'm going to go check out the rest of your creation. You sure you don't need me for anything else? No hiccups at all this morning?"

"There are always hiccups. It's all in how you manage them. That's not for you to worry about today. Breathe would you?"

I look at Tim.

"Did you two call each other this morning?" I say, waving my hand back and forth between the two of them.

"Well, what good is it to bring this grand plan into being," Tim says, "if you aren't going to enjoy it when it's right in front of you?"

"You go enjoy and let me get back to work," Theresa says.

It's now 6:45 and the pink hues of dawn are starting to light the eastern sky. My cell phone rings.

"Hey Sweet Pea, are you getting ready to run?" It's the well worn voice of my friend and book editor, Lynn Skapyak Harlin. My book, *The Good Fight* was her idea. But at first she wasn't exactly thrilled about it. Our initial conversation went something like this.

"Damn, I really don't have time to do this. I'm too busy."

"But you contacted me?"

"I know. I was in bed watching you on the 11 o'clock news. You were talking about your breast cancer foundation and it came to me. Just Bang. *You have to help Donna write her book.*"

"What book?"

"The book you're going to write, dear. Pay attention."

"Okaaay."

It turned out that Lynn's aunt, Evelyn Pinneker had breast cancer. There wasn't much that could be done for her. This was Lynn's way of doing something. Her idea for the book was really a first of its kind. I'd been keeping an online journal, what we'd now refer to as a blog, of my second bout with cancer. More than six thousand viewers had been corresponding with me, many sharing their own stories.

Lynn thought a book about the journal, and the larger point of how we're all connected would make a solid fundraiser for the Donna Foundation. Her publisher, Closet Books, agreed to donate every cent of the proceeds back to DF. We raised hundreds of thousands of dollars and it still brings income to the Foundation today.

We've come a long way with each other since that first conversation. I'm not surprised to hear from her this morning.

"Well, I'm staring at a beautiful dawn right now. We run in about an hour and 45 minutes," I say, looking at my watch.

"That's why I'm calling. Donna, I'm looking at the sky and I swear to God there's a cloud in the shape of a pink ribbon. I've got chills."

"That must be Susan. She's sending us a sign."

I touch the pin on my shirt. We had them made for Susan's funeral on the beach. It's her smiling face with the words "each day's a gift."

"Anyway, I know you're busy, I just wanted to share that with you and tell you good luck today."

"Thanks Lynn."

I return my attention to Theresa.

"Hey T, got a Sharpie?"

She throws me a black marker.

Down one arm I write the name Susan, on the other I write Laurie for my friend Laurie Schellenberg.

"Just a little reminder of what matters," I say. "Thanks for everything T."

She pulls us both into a hug and we're on our way.

We leave the parking lot and it's like stepping out of a back lot at Disney.

Fencing on either side of the road is covered with our running ribbon logo for blocks, and as we make the turn into the pre-race staging area where only runners are allowed, two towering columns announce the entrance to the Runner's Village. White tents with drinks and food and supplies are everywhere. In the distance I can see the vertical alphabet banners marking the area where all the families will meet up with their loved ones once they've finished the race.

And the people! Thousands of runners are already milling around trying to pin on their race numbers, checking the bags that hold the valuables they don't want to carry along the course, stretching, putting Vaseline or Body Glide on the areas of their bodies that might chafe.

Tim gives his bag to the woman at the bag check tent. Then much to her surprise he snatches it back.

"Oh I almost forgot my cowbell!"

We had special pink cowbells made up for the race.

"You want to carry that?"

"Yeah, I think it'll be fun."

"That's a long way to carry a cowbell."

"I'll be fine."

I take off my jacket, stuff it into my bag, and hand it over to the same woman. It is tagged with my race number so it can be easily found when I'm finished running. She looks back at me, incredulous.

"Number one?"

I want to crawl under the tent.

"Yes, that is the number they gave me," I say

"Of course. You're Donna! You look much taller on TV."

"So I've been told."

"Oh, I'll bet people say that to you all the time, don't they?"

"You know what, they do. But that's OK. I have a big chair at work to make me as tall as all the other anchors, so I understand why people think I'm bigger than I am. It's my only chance to be a grown up."

I have given this speech at least five million times in the last 20 years, but I don't mind. This morning it's actually a relief just to make small talk with someone.

"Thanks for volunteering," I say.

"It's a pleasure."

Tim is just standing there looking like he could catch flies in his mouth.

"It's pretty amazing isn't it?" I can hardly believe the scene myself.

"It's beyond amazing Donna," he says, shaking his head.

As we talk, people continue to pour in from the buses.

"We'd better head over to the starting line," I say. "I have announcements to make."

"You go darlin' I'm going to see how well your port-o-lets are working. I haven't had my morning testimonial yet."

"You mean your morning constitutional."

"I always do that, don't I?"

He does. Tim is constantly creating his own phrases. For instance instead of the phrase "mind set" he always says "mind thought." Instead of "all things considered" he says, "all things considering." There are a million of them. He's got his own vocabulary.

He can really come up with some doozies during the newscast. On the set we give him grief about this mercilessly, but it's all in fun.

"Well, it certainly looks like you have your choice of testimonial suites," I say.

One of my pet peeves at marathons is that there are never enough port-o-lets. In this race, where we've registered 75 percent women, I'm not about to skimp. There are little blue houses all over the course and rows of them here at the Runner's Village.

"I'll find you over there. I love you," he says, with a kiss.

I make my way through the throngs of runners, catching pieces of conversation along the way.

"So, we go out slow, OK we need to average an 8 minute pace…"

"I never stop to pee during a race. Once I start running, I'm not stopping until the end."

"How do you attach this timing chip? I can't get it to stay even on my shoelaces."

It's so much fun watching all these runners do what runners do.

Back out into the crowd of spectators, I set my sights on the start line.

Someone taps me on the shoulder. A woman wearing a pink bandanna.

"Excuse me, you're Donna right?"

"Yes."

"Well, I'm Donna too. And I'm a survivor. I just wanted to say thank you for starting this race."

"Well, it's your race too. How are you doing?"

"I'm only a cheerleader today. I'm in treatment now. But I'll be running next year."

"Hang in there. Your treatment will be done before you know it. I'll look forward to having you in the race next February. Thanks for being here today, though, we need cheerleaders," I say.

I have corresponded with at least a half a dozen Donnas on email since the race was made public. Some just wanted to buy a shirt because it said "Donna." But I've spoken with a number of survivor Donnas as well. I like the notion that it's everyone's race. That's how I want every runner to feel.

At the start line Jeff is standing on a stage to the west of where the elite runners will line up. He is already making announcements, thanking sponsors, giving people advice about the heat. When he's finished he hands the microphone to me.

"Donna this is really something. Can you believe all the people?"

"Yes, I can," I say, and I mean it.

I don't know how, but from the very beginning I just knew this was going to go and go big. From the moment the light bulb first came on in my head that morning with Edith, I just knew. I could see all of this in vivid detail in my head. It didn't matter how many people told me it couldn't be done, and many did. I never doubted for an instant that Jeff and I would be standing right here in front of thousands of people ready to run the first and only marathon dedicated to the cause of breast cancer.

"So what pace are you planning to run today?" Jeff asks.

"Oh I just want to finish, Jeff I'm not even thinking of a pace."

"You're going to run the half marathon, right?"

"I still don't know. I don't suspect I will know until sometime out there on the course. My number says marathon."

I point to the line on my race bib that refers to marathon or half marathon status. I registered for the race long before my latest diagnosis and surgery.

I already know Jeff's feelings about this. They are the same as Joanie's.

"What pace are you planning to run today?" I ask moving right along.

"Well Barb (Jeff's wife) and I are going to run one and ones."

That's Galloway language for run a minute walk a minute.

"That should bring us to the finish line in about five hours."

"Wow, I would have expected longer with one and ones."

"Well, when we walk, we don't stroll, and when we run, we get after it pretty good," he says making a zooming motion with his hand.

It is now around 8 a.m. We are about 30 minutes from the start of the race. The elites are beginning to make their way to the start line. The Kenyans are already running to warm up. Keith, who is in charge of making sure only the elites get into this front corral, is watching them too. Our eyes meet briefly and he gives me a thumbs up.

The Jacksonville Jaguars cheerleaders, the Roar, are getting the crowd revved up on the sidelines and posing for pictures. Jaguars owners Wayne and Delores Weaver are there, watching their every move. I'm touched to see them here. I called Delores early on in the planning process and asked for her advice and support. She and Wayne have played a huge role in raising funds for breast cancer research at Dana Farber in Boston. Delores lost her mom to breast cancer and she and Wayne have helped raise millions to find a cure. I ran the Boston Marathon for Dana Farber in 1999, ironically just months before my first diagnosis. Every year, the Weavers travel to Boston to support the runners. So to see them out here today is a wonderful affirmation.

"Time to welcome everyone, Donna," Jeff says. "I've already thanked the sponsors."

Jeff introduces me and I step to the microphone.

I'm really here. Soak it in, Donna.

"Good morning everyone, welcome to the inaugural 26.2 With Donna, The National Marathon to Fight Breast Cancer. I have to tell you this morning that I am blown away by the scene in front of me. You all have come here from every state in the nation and 15 countries to help us finish breast cancer and to run for those who need our help. I want to take this opportunity to say thank you to Jeff Galloway, who has prepared so many of you to run today. And Dr. Edith Perez, my doctor and the brilliant researcher here at the Mayo Clinic who is going to help us find a cure for this disease. Without Jeff and Edith, we would have never made it to the starting line. I look forward to the day when we can announce that right here in Jacksonville, Florida we have found the cure. And then folks, we can just run for fun. Thank you from the bottom of my heart for participating in our inaugural race. You will find one of the warmest, most supportive crowds in the world along your journey. Have a great day, and I'll see you on the road!"

I thank Jeff, and the Mayo dignitaries who are there at the stage and walk over to speak to Wayne and Delores.

"This is such a wonderful surprise," I say hugging them both. "I am so honored to have you here."

"Donna, we wouldn't be anywhere else," Delores says, her eyes glowing brown bulbs.

"This is very impressive," Wayne adds. "It's hard to believe this is a first year event."

"Well we must be official now that you two are here. I appreciate your blessings, and it's great to have The Roar here too."

"You are more than welcome," Delores says.

I say my goodbyes and pop into the VIP tent to the east of the start line. Julie is standing there talking with her brother Craig. Both are running.

"Can you believe I am actually going to run?" Julie says.

"You are just repaying a bet," I say. I can't resist the reminder.

Julie was so sure we'd never get the marathon idea together that she promised, "The day you do, I'll sign up to run." And to her credit, she did. She's worked hard and though she won't admit it, I think she's really excited.

My best pal Andrea Cole is here too. As usual she looks like she just stepped off the pages of a modeling magazine. Andrea has never run a step in her life before all of this. Loyal to the core, she's doing this for me.

My tall Greek goddess of a friend always makes a statement with her look.

"Are you going to run, or pose," I joke.

"Is there a rule against looking good while you run?" she says flipping her black curls at me.

"I haven't found a way to do it yet," I say. "But you do look great."

"I'm actually pretty proud of myself," she says.

And she should be. Andrea has always had the perfect body. Even in college when the rest of us were gaining our freshman 15, she could eat anything and everything and never gain a pound. And her body is sculpted like she lifts weights, but the only thing she lifts is that sandwich (don't hold the mayo) to her mouth. For the past six months she's been training hard to finish the half marathon.

"I'm proud of you too, Sweetie. Have fun out there today," I say.

"You have fun too," she says, putting her hands on my shoulders and locking her enormous brown eyes on mine. "Make sure you open your eyes and see everything today. This is your day. I want you to love it." She reaches down and hugs me so tightly I think I may lose another rib.

Andrea is almost 5' 9". All heart.

I step outside, and make a bee line for that gorgeous guy in the pink headband waiting for me at the starting line.

Tim is looking at me just beaming. His eyes are wet with emotion.

"Look at all of this," he says. "Donna, this is beautiful."

"OK, break it up, break it up."

I turn to see my pahdnah in crime Nancy Bauer striding up next to me.

"Well aren't you just a hot shit," she says grinning from ear to ear. "This is wicked cool."

Edith walks up right behind her.

"Edith, you remember my friend Nancy Bauer," I say.

"Of course Nancy, good to see you again. I didn't know you were running the marathon."

"I'm not. Donna and I are running the half marathon, right princess?" She turns to me and squints her eyes.

I look at Edith.

"What do you think Edith? Joanie and Jeff are both worried about my immune system if I run the whole way. You're the doctor. What do you say?"

"Donna, look around you this morning. Can you feel the emotions from these people? So much love out here and so much hope. I can't imagine anything that could be better for your immune system. If you want to run the whole way, do it."

I look at Nancy. She looks from Edith to me.

"Well, I'm running the half," she says confidently.

"Fine," I say.

"Ladies and gentleman, our National Anthem," the announcer says.

As the song begins, Edith starts to cry and once she starts, she can't stop. She is standing there, my doctor and my friend, who has spent her entire professional life trying to solve this terrible illness, and the power of the moment just hits her like a downburst in a storm. I, on the other hand, am so proud that I can't wipe this love sick goofy grin off my face for anything. So here we stand, Edith sobbing, me grinning, with our arms wrapped around each other listening to the National Anthem.

The singer exits the stage and the countdown begins.

"Runners on your mark," Jeff yells.

"Get set."

Then the cannon sounds and we are all drenched in a shower of pink confetti.

"And we're off and running in the first ever national marathon to end breast cancer," Jeff shouts. He raises his hand triumphantly in the air.

19 | Hope Floats

This is one of those moments in life that almost seems to go in slow motion. I remember when my daughter Danielle was three. We bought her a swing set for the back yard. I still see her sitting at the top of the slide giggling, the sun creating a crown of light around her curly brown hair. She's in a sky blue outfit. The top has ruffled sleeves. The pants are covered with drawings of apples and pears. Her stubby toddler toes are wiggling with delight.

Stay just like this.

What a picture. I wanted to freeze her in time right there. It's the same now.

I glance toward the sideline. Tears roll freely from Delores' eyes. She makes no attempt to dry them. Can't quite gauge her expression. Happy? Sad? Both perhaps. The crowd surges and we all move together streaming toward the bridge that will take us to our route along the ocean.

"Howdy Donna!"

It's Bob Stephens. He's with the Austin, Texas Galloway group. They brought about 30 people to run including their training director, Will

Carlson. This is Will's 50th marathon. Jeff and I visited there for their training kick-off several months ago.

"My little group within the group is called Bob's Babes," he told me. "We have a special theme for the race but you'll have to wait and see what it is."

Now I see.

"Check it out," he says, pointing to the words on his shirt.

Texans for ta-tas! This is a crew that knows how to enjoy themselves.

"Love it Bob! You and the babes have fun, OK?"

"We always do," he says and takes off into a throng of runners.

We reach the top of the bridge and the Jacksonville Sheriff's Office helicopter is hovering overhead. I picture Barry clicking away up there trying to get the perfect shot.

Off to the right, in the Intracoastal Waterway, the Jacksonville Fire Rescue Department has it's boat spewing fountains of water everywhere. Runners point and applaud as they pass, and wave at the chopper overhead.

Tim touches my arm.

"Look."

I follow his eyes back into the crowd.

There it is. The picture of my dreams.

People, as far as I can see. A ribbon of pink and white, streaming from Mayo over the bridge behind me.

A photographer in a pink bandanna runs up ahead of us and waits for us to run by.

Click . . . click . . . click

Drew, Danielle, Donna and Tim in Costa Rica.

Amanda Napolitano training the troops.

Jonathan Oliff, Tim Deegan, Phil Clark, Kurtis Loftus at marathon training.

These are the Deegans in the volcanic mud in Costa Rica.

Amanda Napolitano and Chris Twiggss, our Galloway team leaders.

Donna shooting her weekly running journal for First Coast News.

Tim with San Jose Episcopal Day School students after their run.

Donna and Shannon Ogden goofing around on the First Coast News set.

Donna and her mother, Elizabeth Hazouri the day before the inaugural race.

Debra Sullins, a DF recipient, showing her gratitude at the inaugural race.

Andrea Cole with thumbs up- She makes it look glam on the beach.

Tim, Julie Terrazzono and Jim Gilmore at the finish line of the inaugural race.

Dr. Edith Perez and Donna share an emotional moment before the start of the inaugural race.

Pink confetti showers the runners at the start line.

Drew, Kamryn and Matt Deegan, cheering on the beach at the inaugural race.

Donna gives Tim a victory hug after the race.

Joan Benoit Samuelson and Donna after the 2009 marathon.

Danielle, Andrea, and Donna at the finish 2009.

The Deegan, Barnett, and Hazouri clans together at a pre-race day brunch.

Fans cheer on the runners from a balcony.

Jeff Galloway at the Pre-race Galloway pep rally.

Tim Deegan, Nancy Bauer, Donna Deegan and fellow runners at the start of the 2008 race.

Love Banner- one of many signed by runners on the "memorial mile."

Amanda Napolitano and John TenBroek at the VIP party the Friday before the inaugural race.

Dr. Edith Perez, Tim Deegan, Dale Hansen, and Donna approaching mile 20.

Galloway Pacers lead runners through the beach portion of the race

Pink Spiderman crosses the
bridge in the 2009 marathon.

Donna thanks Drew with a kiss after he places
her finisher's medal around her neck.

A "super" finish for these two heroes.

Kurtis Loftis at his Why I'm Running Booth at
the Inaugural Expo Feb. 2008.

Tara Hazouri, David Barnett, Lindsay Haselden and Mary Haselden, after finishing the
inaugural race.

Bob Stephens of Bob's Babes. He brought a group from Austin Texas and named their team Texans for Ta-Tas.

Ike Brown high fiving onlookers.

Dr. Zhi Huo, happy as always.

Donna and her uncle David Barnett after both completed the inaugural race.

Publisher, George Gilpatrick, editor, Lynn Skapyak Harlin, and graphic designer, Oscar Senn, my Closet Books fearless team.

It's Tom White. A Jacksonville Police detective who runs with our training group. Tom and his wife Becky take pictures for the community photo section of Jacksonville.com, the website for our local newspaper. They also chronicle all of our team training runs and generously donate all the pictures back to us.

"You get that bridge shot Tom?" I shout, as I pass him by.

"About a hundred," he yells back. Tom will run the entire marathon with that camera in tow.

We exit the bridge on the cloverleaf and run north on A1A toward the beach.

Be there. Be there.

Over and over in my head I am willing the crowd support I've been promising to all these runners. People at the beaches are notorious for supporting athletic events. I've done my best to get the word out. Taken out ads in the newspaper, given community talks. Theresa even asked her friend Troy Winn to head up a community outreach group that went door to door along the race route asking for support. But it is early, and it's Sunday morning, so I really don't know what to expect.

"Hey look," Nancy says, pointing to the ground in front of us. Every few yards there is a large pink running ribbon to mark the race route.

"It's pink chalk. The crews went out overnight and lined the entire route," I say.

We hang a right on 37th Street and my heart almost stops in my chest.

People are lined up three or four deep along the road. They're ringing cowbells, clapping thunder sticks, playing Chariots of Fire. Instant waterworks. I can hardly catch my breath. Have to take little gulps of air just to keep from hyperventilating.

Tim waves to them all, swinging the cowbell so vigorously he almost takes my head off.

The road bends to flank the ocean and the sea of people expands. Everywhere spectators are holding signs. "Thank you for running for me!" "Go Mom, you can do it!" "Do your best for the breast!"

Many houses are flying our flags with the words "We Support 26.2 With Donna." A huge banner draped across road from one balcony to another says "Go Runners, You Rock!"

We are nearing the five mile mark. Almost time to hit the sand.

"Woo hoo! Yea! Go Donnaah!"

Victoria Ogden, my evening co-anchor's wife, is screaming at the top of her lungs, jumping up and down in her Chuck Taylor's holding a sign that says "Fit Club Loves Donna." An inside joke that began months ago when we each decided to buy a Honda Fit.

Now I'm laughing. Mostly I'm floating, just like Keith said. I literally do not feel my feet touching the ground. Gliding along on a cloud of joy and love and hope. I may burst with pride. I thank every person I can as we run by, inhaling the energy of the crowd.

A right turn at 16th Avenue South takes us across the mats that lead to the hard packed sands of our First Coast beaches. The sky is clear. The ocean, a sparkling blue green mirror. Some runners stop, pull out their cameras and phones and start taking pictures of themselves and each other on the beach.

A large raucous group to our right is just going nuts. It's Tim's family. His sister Mary Pat, her son David. His parents Margie and Paul. Tim's brother Dan whose wife Robin is running the race. Their kids Brian, Haley and Kyle, and Tim's other brother Mike and his wife Kim along with their five kids Kamryn, Drew, Matthew, Luke and Ava. Whew, what a crew! We run to them, high-fiving everyone as we pass.

Every half a mile or so since we started Nancy has been asking me how I'm doing.

"You know I'm turning around at the half marathon point, right?"

"Yes, Nancy I know."

"So are you going with me, or what, because I'm not running the whole thing."

"Yes, Nancy, I know."

"I mean it Donna."

"OK, Nancy."

We pass the historic Jacksonville Beach lifeguard station. A smooth white building with a tower that has a red cross painted near the top. The lifeguards are standing outside cheering us down the beach. The salt air tastes good. A plane flies by with a banner that reads "Finish Breast Cancer."

It's decision time. We are nearing the Jacksonville Beach Pier. Nancy has stopped asking. Here at the six and a half mile point the half marathoners will leave the beach and take the road back to the Mayo Clinic, while the full marathoners will run another mile along the sand and then continue the journey on into Neptune and Atlantic Beach.

I see the signs as we make our approach. Volunteers are waving the half marathoners off the beach. To my left I see my colleagues. Phil Amato, Patty Crosby, Deanna Fené and the rest of the group from First Coast

News are there waiting to be my tag team. This is where I turn back and they relay the rest of the 26.2 miles as a gesture of support.

"So what are you thinking there sweetheart?" Tim asks.

"I feel really good Tim. I don't even feel like I've run a mile, much less almost seven."

"Seven is a lot less than 26 Donna. There would be no shame at all in doing the half. You finish feeling good and you welcome everyone back in."

Nancy is being conspicuously quiet.

"I know but there will never be another inaugural race. I said I would go on how I feel and I feel great."

"If you want to go I'm with you. I just want you to be sure."

I turn to Nancy.

"I know we're running the whole damn thing."

"Nancy you don't have to do it. I completely understand if you want to turn back. You have Boston to worry about. It will not hurt my feelings at all."

"I didn't fly all the way down here to leave you. Let's go."

I run over to my friends from the station and give each of them a big hug.

"I love you guys for being here. I'm going to finish the race."

"I knew it," says Patty, shaking her head and laughing.

"Have a great run, Donna," says Deanna.

"You go girl," adds Phil.

They give a cheer as we continue down the beach.

"OK, marathon mama, we need a strategy here," Tim says. "Do you want to do three and ones like your group does in training or do you want to bust it down to two and ones."

I have literally been so mesmerized by the crowd that taking walk breaks hasn't even occurred to me.

"Let's start running three and walking one and see how that goes," I say. "Nancy, can you call the walk breaks? If Tim does it he'll start staring at the weather and forget when it's time and it won't be pretty."

"You betcha," she says.

"Mind if I join you?" A tall woman in a wig made of pink feathers is running beside me. It's Paula Bacon, the Galloway training director in Albany, Georgia.

"Paula, hey, great to see you! Of course."

"I'm hurting today. I was going to run the whole marathon, then I had an injury, so I was just going to run the half. But as soon as I saw all these people… Oh my gosh Donna this is awesome! This is the most inspirational race I've ever done. You are going to have 20,000 people here next year. I'm going to try to go the whole way, but I promise not to slow you down."

"I'm not sure humans can run much slower than I'm running today, Paula, so not much chance of that," I say.

The crowds seem to get rowdier as we go. Back on the road in Neptune Beach the whole street is decked out with pink ribbons on the trees and people having block parties. At Pete's Bar some people are holding out beers for the runners.

"Don't do it Tim. Too far to go," I say. "We're just coming up on mile nine."

"It's tempting," he says, ringing his cowbell in the direction of the gold filled cups.

"Should I call an audible? Bar Break? What do you think Tim?" Nancy asks. He looks back at me and I shake my head.

"Better wait, maybe they'll still be here on the way back," he says.

Deep into Atlantic Beach, up the hill toward 19th Street, people are hanging off their balconies, our friend Josie is playing the bongo drums in her front yard. The ocean winks at me on the right as we begin the descent toward 20th. A left hand turn and down Seminole Road, we stride past Susan's house.

"Hey girl, awesome job today on the weather," I say touching my smiling Susan pin.

"Oh Lord Tim, Susan would be so happy to see all this."

"She's watching, Donna and I'm sure she is happy," he says.

At mile 12 we join up with our friend Jim Gilmore. We're actually right down the street from his house.

"What in God's name are you wearing?" I ask staring at his long dark running tights. Are you nuts? It's hot out here."

"Perhaps an error in judgment," he agrees. "I am getting pretty warm, but I'm trying not to focus on that. My neighbors are doing a great job aren't they?"

We are nearing the halfway point in the race. Mile 13, and Jim is right. The folks in Atlantic Beach have simply outdone themselves. There are homemade aid stations everywhere. Kids are handing out fruit. One woman holds a sign that says "You're running for my mom, a 9 year survivor!" Another sign says "Go Runners, We Love YOU!" Shouts of encouragement are constant.

There are bands, and chalk drawings on the road. The yards are decked out in pink.

"Hey how about an ice cold cloth?"a man yells, pulling a few from his cooler.

Each of us grabs one.

Ahhhh

I soak my head and then wrap the cloth around the back of my neck. It's a welcome relief.

Temperatures are now climbing toward 70 and it is warm, but beautiful.

"Let's Rock and Roll," says Nancy. This is her way to announce that each walk break is over and that it's time to run.

Mile 14 and we make the turn for home. The beautiful live oaks of Selva Marina offer some shady relief from the late morning sun.

"So Tim, what do you think the dew point is right now?"

"Well, let's see…"

Tim launches into a long explanation of what the dew point is, and the statistical reasons for this, the average dew point this time of year, and the physiological effects on the body of dew point. This is my strategy when I start to get tired. I don't want to have to talk anymore, so I ask Tim a weather question. Once, he actually went for 37 minutes on isobars and I didn't have to say a word.

Mile 18 and we are nearing Bay Street in Neptune Beach. Kids zig and zag on skateboards and girls in bathing suits lounge in beach chairs blasting their radios and cheering us along as we pass. The smell of sun tan oil is thick in the air. It all reminds me of a Gary Mack painting. But I'm not sure that even our most famous local artist could have imagined a scene this perfect.

I am getting deep into my own head now. Chemo and shredded feet aside, it's that time in the race when my body usually signals me that it's time to stop. In fact it's rather insistent.

Hello? Anybody listening here? I've run quite far enough, thank you and I don't care what you say, I'm going to sit down . . . Now!

"I'm going to have to switch to two and ones guys," I say.

"You got it," says Nancy.

Nancy adjusts her watch and we march on in silence. We are all dealing with our own demons. Even Tim, who would normally be finishing the race about now is exhausted. It's been a long emotional week and his body is simply not used to being out on the course for this long.

Mile 20 now and we pass the Seawalk Pavillion in Jacksonville Beach. Our friend Dane Jefferys and his band Scholar's Word are playing their unique brand of Reggae on the main stage. On either side of the street a faux brick wall appears. "The Pink Wall" symbolizes breaking through the barriers to find a cure.

The fact that we chose mile 20 for this, is no mistake. It's often said that a marathon is really two races. The first 20 miles and the last six. This is where the body tends to hit its limits. Every runner knows that there is joy on the other side of that wall, and triumph. But at mile 20 the body isn't buying that bill of goods.

I'm done I tell you! I can't do it. I won't. My legs are cramping. I can't put another thing in my stomach. I'm not going to move my feet. Stop stop stop!

It takes every bit of mental strength I have to stay focused on the goal.

Just finish baby.

"How far to the bridge?"

I ask this question, having designed this course myself and knowing every inch of it.

"Less than four miles," Tim says.

Did he say four or four hundred?

"I'm going to have to walk some, guys. You go ahead," Jim says.

"Are you sure Jim? We'll wait for you," I offer.

"No, no, I'll see you at the finish line," he insists and we move on.

Barely hear the cheers around me now. They sound distant, like I'm listening through cotton balls in my ears. A woman runs out from the crowd to hug me and nearly knocks me off my feet.

"You are running for my mother," she says. "Thank you so much."

This gives me some momentary juice. Somewhere in my increasingly fuzzy brain, I remember why I'm out here and my mind is detoured for a time from the pain in my legs and the sting of the sweat in my eyes.

We stop for water near mile 22 and Brad Winkler and his Bishop Kenny High School volunteers shout words of encouragement.

"You're almost there. Just a few miles left!"

Despite the protests from my stomach, I down a final packet of GU energy gel and say a silent prayer that it will get me where I need to go.

Finally, we make the turn at the base of the bridge. It hardly seems like the same structure we ran over five hours ago.

"This bridge isn't supposed to be steep," I say. "Who took my bridge and replaced it with the Empire State Building?"

"Once we're up the ramp, it will level out, Donna," Tim says. "Why don't we just take it easy up the ramp?"

"OK, let's walk it, after that I'll need to drop to one and ones."

I am completely spent, but very faintly in the back of my mind, a little voice is beginning to build. It hasn't yet drowned out the 'I can't' screamers, but I can hear my inner Kenyan trying to speak out.

Only two miles to go baby. Just two miles and you're home. The finish line is waiting for you. The victory is just over the hill. Go Go Go!

"Tim, just get me to the top of that bridge, OK? I have to finish this race."

"That was never in question pahdnah," Nancy says. "We didn't come this far to give up."

"We're all going to finish," says Paula. "Donna, running with you all today, it's the only reason I'm going to make it. And you are going to make it too. We're almost there."

My sister- in- law Robin runs up beside us and so does a man named Bill Hart. I recognize him as a friend of Andrea's. He's raised a ton of money for us, more than 10,000 dollars.

"Hey, look who it is," says Robin, looking at me. "I'm running with Donna!" That's the line we use in our on air promotions, so she's tweaking me a little.

As it turns out, Robin has slowed down to help a friend who is struggling. Bill's hurting too. We are all trying to somehow will our bodies to the top of the bridge. Individually our energy is sapped, collectively we have enough to power each other.

Finally, the pavement begins to level, and we are there!

"There's the finish line!" I can see it in the distance.

Oh yea!

Everyone lets out a cheer.

"Let's go claim that awesome medal," Paula says.

A surge of adrenaline sends a blast of energy to my legs. New life. The finish. I've seen it in my mind, and now it's there in front of me. I let the momentum take me. My legs fly down the back side of the bridge. It's no longer an effort to turn them, they are turning all by themselves. My hands look like sausages, but I have yet to feel my swollen feet. The most beat up part of my body hasn't been an issue all day.

We round the turn to San Pablo Road and I hear Dr. John calling out the finishers' names on the loud speakers.

"We understand that Donna and Tim Deegan are on the home stretch," he yells.

The crowds on the roadside roar encouragement as we pass, shaking pink pom-poms, ringing cowbells and calling our names.

Tim rings his cowbell right back at them and we pick up the pace.

Three hundred yards, two hundred, one hundred. We're sprinting.

The clock flashes 5 hours and 51 minutes. The elites finished three and a half hours ago, but in my mind I am a Kenyan in full stride.

Tim grabs my hand and raises it in triumph as we streak across the finish line together, with Nancy, Paula, Robin and Bill all around us. Jeff Galloway places a medal around my neck and my pain evaporates into a state of pure bliss.

Hugs descend on me from everywhere. First my kids, then Edith, who apparently finished minutes before me.

"Way to go Mom," says Danielle.

"I can't believe you actually just ran 26 miles," Drew says.

"Don't forget the .2," I say.

"You did it girl," Edith says grinning like only she can. "Feeling good?"

"It got a little warm out there at the end, but I can't complain. Having only trained up to 13 miles, my body did extraordinarily well. And my feet didn't bother me a bit, despite those lovely pink pills you have me taking. How was it for you?"

"Fabulous! I loved it. The people along the course were amazing. Donna we have started something very special here. I think the whole clinic really understands now how powerful this is."

"Have you checked with your folks in the medical tent? Is everyone OK?"

"We had one serious heat reaction. But she's going to be fine. I don't have a lot of details. All in all, it was a great day out there. We'll follow up later. Go enjoy your family. They are all waiting to see you."

Andrea, Julie, my sister Tara, my Aunts Evelyn and Mary and Mary's daughter Lindsay, all completed the half marathon. I greet them all with hugs and congratulations.

"I'm doing the full, next year," Tara says.

"Me too," says Mary.

"David!" My mom's brother is there too.

"I knew you were going to run the whole thing," he says. "And once I knew you were doing it, I had to do it too."

"I hoped you would. How was it?"

"It was great, really fun. But take a look at my feet."

I look down and David is wearing two different running shoes.

"What? Couldn't decide which pair to wear?"

"No, I just never checked them before I got dressed this morning. Apparently this is all I packed," he says, rolling his eyes.

"Well how did that work out for you?"

"My feet are sore, although I guess they would be anyway. I feel a little foolish, but I finished."

"And it just makes it a better story to tell for years to come," I say.

A volunteer hands me a bag of ice. I am sore in so many places I have no idea where to put it so I just plop it on top of my head.

Loud hoots and cheers turn my focus back to the finish line.

A group of pink wigged women is finishing together, holding hands and practically dancing across the mats.

Every few seconds more runners cross, each writing their own stories. Some pump their fists in victory, others burst into tears. Everyone seems to have a sense of why we are here. All the joy of surviving, all the sadness of loss, all the hopes for the future, they are laid bare here for all to see and it binds us.

Finally after the last runner has stepped across the line, I take one last look around. I'm exhausted, but there is a part of me that doesn't want to leave. There's something magical that happened here today and I'm not anxious to lift the spell.

"You'd better take me home soon, or you are going to have to carry me," I say to Tim. Using each other for support, we limp off happily toward the car.

20 | Boiling it Down

March 7, 2008

I drop some pasta into the pot and watch it disappear into the boiling water.

Tim is stretched out on the couch reading a book.

"Do you want to skip the tomato sauce since we're running tomorrow?"

Tim likes to keep it simple the night before he runs.

"Sure, a little butter or olive oil works fine for me," he says, glancing up from the reading glasses perched on the tip of his nose.

"It looks like they are going to have another record attendance for the River Run this year," I say.

"That's good to hear. Hey, thanks for picking up my race packet. Were there a lot of people at the expo?"

"A ton. As a matter of fact, I ran into Linda White and her mother-in-law. Man, she looks amazing."

"Linda, or her mother-in-law?"

"Well both actually, but Johnny's mom is 61 now. Tim, she is in better shape than most 20 year olds. You should see this woman's arms. She's ripped."

"Well she was a national swimming champion you know, and she wins her age group all the time in the River Run. The whole family is so athletic. Johnny was a professional mountain bike racer before his pancreatitis. He's in his 40's now and seems completely recovered, back to his prime," Tim says.

"Yes, that's what I was going to tell you. Remember the doctor that Loretta Haycook wanted me to see? Well, Linda just raved about her tonight and everything she did for Johnny. I think I'm going to go ahead and make an appointment with her. Linda's going to send me her phone number. In fact, she said she'd do it as soon as she got home. Mind if I check my email before we eat?

"Sure, unless you're going to look up in two hours and say, 'Oh where has the time gone,'" he says.

"I'll just read that one," I promise. "We have a few minutes before the pasta is ready anyway."

Just as she'd said, Linda had sent me all I needed to know about Dr. Bridget Freeman.

Hey Donna,

It was good talking with you at the River Run Expo today. Here is the info about the DR. Johnny went/goes to. Her name is Bridget Freeman, MD. Her office is located in The Sanctuary in San Marco at 1617 Thacker Road . Bridget uses her intuitive healing gift to decide what therapies you may need to balance your body into being able to heal itself. Johnny is a very practical person but, at that point he was willing to try anything. After firsthand witnessing the changes in himself not only physically but mentally/emotionally , he would just laugh when she treated him with her "voodoo"(as he jokingly called it). So, I think he became more receptive to her treatments and that in itself helped him. Plus, he felt that HE was doing something in his recovery.

Anyways, back to your situation . . . I think it would be a positive thing for you to call her just to talk and see if now is the right time for you to meet with her. I did give Bridget a call and let her know I would be passing on her info to you. Please let me know if you need anything else or if you would like to know more about Johnny's treatments, etc . . .

I am so glad you asked me about this today. I felt that you two needed to meet awhile ago. And you have been in my thoughts lately (due to the marathon then being consumed by your book "The Good Fight") so, I hope this all works out.

Faith, Hope, Love and Laughter-

Linda White

The note ends with Dr. Freeman's phone number.

"Well that was quick. She's a sweet woman. They've been through a lot," I say.

"Johnny was close to death at one point wasn't he?"

"Yes, he actually had something called idiopathic chronic pancreatitis. That basically means they had no idea why he had it, what caused it or how to cure it. He was having severe attacks every few weeks and long stays in the hospital. He had been to a number of specialists all of whom threw up their hands. That went on for a couple of years. Finally he was told that some sort of islet pancreas cell transplant was his only hope for survival. So they were waiting on insurance approval when they met Dr. Freeman. She put him on IV vitamin C, acupuncture, healing energy work, yoga, and nutritional counseling. They were hoping to just get him strong enough for the transplant. But he just got so much better they dropped the idea of the surgery altogether. As you said, look at Johnny now, he's back to full speed."

"No problems at all?"

"Nothing that keeps him from living his life the way he likes too. He has an occasional mild flare up maybe once a year, and Linda says he recovers so quickly he doesn't have to be hospitalized."

"Dr. Freeman definitely sounds like someone we should meet. If you make an appointment, I'll go with you."

"Great, I'll do it first thing Monday morning."

We eat our dinner, discussing strategy for what time we'll get up, when to leave for the race, how we'll find each other afterward.

"Five a.m. will be here in a blink, so I think I'm just going to head to bed and read for a while until I fall asleep," Tim says.

"Sounds good. I'm going to go through some of the feedback emails from the marathon and pull a few for this month's newsletter. Amanda needs them by Monday, and since we have the night off, I might as well go for it tonight. Plus I need to write a thank you to the runners, and I can't seem to come up with the right words. I've probably written it a million times."

"OK, race queen, but we took the night off for a reason. You'll want fresh legs tomorrow. Don't stay up too late."

I kiss Tim goodnight and dive into the thousands of confections I've received in our post race survey. This is more fun than a human being should be allowed to have. Picking out favorites is the hard part. Finally I settle on a handful and complete a final draft thanking the runners who participated in our inaugural marathon.

Hello Friends!

I have written and rewritten this letter so many times and I still can't seem to find adequate words to thank all of you who participated in our inaugural 26.2 with Donna The National Marathon to Fight Breast Cancer.

I have literally received thousands of emails since the race. As I have since day one I am doing my best to answer every one. Your encouragement has been amazing and I know you will agree it was returned to you ten-fold by the crowds who lined the race route in Jacksonville and our beautiful beach communities. I'm not sure it is possible to feel a greater sense of pride in our mission and our event than I do today.

I hope you will take the time to read some of the feedback we received on the race. We've attached a number of excerpts and you will see a common theme. I think we all made a lot of new friends. We also took the first critical steps of our personal journey to FINISH BREAST CANCER. I am certain I have never been more satisfied to cross the finish line of any marathon than I was to cross it with you. Read on.

Well organized and run race. Everything from the transportation, parking, Expo, race course, and water breaks was excellent! ... Don't change a thing.

Michael Meece

>>>>

Greatest day ever--What a fantastic job! . . . hope to do it again next Feb. when I will be 81! Everybody was a class act!

Sincerely,

Marie Gier

>>>>

Thank you for all of your work putting on this great event. I loved every minute of the training with the Galloway group runs, making new running friends, the cause, your inspiration, the brownie in the race packet, the race logo in chalk on the course, the supporters, all of the volunteers and finally, my supportive family with my little girl wearing her pink "Go" shirt and my son wearing his white "Mom!" shirt.

Linda

>>>>

What an amazing time we had! Thank you so much for all the fabulous organization with this event for such a worthy cause. We have participated in 14 Marathons and 4 Half Marathons and this one jumped to the top of the list.

DD

>>>>

What you and Dr. Perez and Jeff Galloway and all your committees were able to organize and accomplish was HUGE. I know you realize this, but I don't think you can fathom how deeply you have touched me, and I'm sure others like me. I am 48 years old and consider myself to be a strong, active person (mother--2 teenagers now, wife, friend, dedicated worker, etc) mentally, physically, spiritually, and emotionally, yet I am weakened internally by this disease that lurks within my body, trying to shut it down. It has been trying for nearly 13 years now, and guess what--I just ran the first national 1/2 marathon for breast cancer! ...

LOVED running on the beach. Never forget what a gift the beach and ocean is for walks and jogs. I've been wearing 3-4 layers of clothing for my training runs all winter! . . .

You are very special. You are a gift that came into the lives of so many people at a time when we needed it and appreciate it. So thank you, from the bottom of my heart.

Steph Lesiecki

>>>>

That really was an impressive marathon! I will recommend it to anyone that asks. The beach section was beautiful. Congrats on one of the best organized first time marathons.

Connie Gardner

>>>>

The organization and execution was first class and the community really stepped up to the plate.

Usually first time events have several issues come up but your team of organizers did a first class job.

Constance Frankenberg

>>>>

For an inaugural marathon . . .

-- a most scenic course

-- great fan support throughout Jax Beach, Neptune Beach and Atlantic Beach

    -- great volunteers

    -- well organized

    -- great cause

    -- great finishers medal

    -- a pleasure to run part of the race with Donna and Tim

Jacksonville now has a premier marathon event. See you in 2009.

bruce reid

>>>>

You can put this marathon up with any of the big ones, no questions asked. You can feel proud that a majority of those runners who have participated in major marathons would feel the same way. I have never been part of a running event where all along the course people were thanking me for running. Yes, at Boston, New York, Chicago, Marine Corps, etc. there are throngs of spectators everywhere cheering you on, but not with the sincerity and enthusiasm that I experienced on Sunday.

Charles Lechner

>>>>

WOW!! You sure can put on a great run!! My friends and I ran and all agreed how awesome it was!! The support was amazing. Besides a million volunteers, all the neighborhood people out in support was unbelievable. How nice to be greeted by cheers, food, and much needed water hoses. I felt like a champ as I was running. The organizers did a fine job. And all the volunteers were super. You rock!!!

Hc

>>>>

Congratulations and Thank You for a great race! The warmth and welcome I felt from your community was overwhelming. I could not believe so many were out there cheering us on. It was an incredible experience!!

April Hill

>>>>

I don't know who to or even how to express my gratitude but I am forever grateful for everything including the full 26.2 miles of enthusiastic people cheering me on and thanking me for running for their mother, grandmother and sisters. I felt like a rock star and it made a memory that will last forever! Thank you.

Dana Beller

>>>>

I LOVED this race!! I have run inaugural races before and I must say, you all were very well organized. I was very impressed from the expo, shuttles, and the race was amazing and flowed very well. I loved all the pink and especially working hard to get that beautiful medal. This was my 10th Half Marathon and it is my most favorite because of the beach, the medal and of course the cause. My grandmother died of breast cancer and I love that you all can put on such a great race and give so much back to the cause. Thank you for a great experience and I'll see you next year!!

Amy Duck

>>>>

Having complete strangers thank me for running for them/their mothers/their friends, seeing people struggle through an exceptionally hot day but pushing on for their loved ones, and spectators adding their own aid stations with hoses, Gatorade, popsicles, and kind words of encouragement was enough to touch my heart in a way I didn't expect.

Secondly, this race was literally run to perfection. The expo was terrific, friendly people, and no lines. Race morning was smooth, the bus service was fast, and the port-o-lets... how can I put this? There were NO LINES!!! It was like every runners dream. During the race, the attention to detail was evident as well. Fully stocked aid stations, terrific cheering sections, and the flooring added to the soft sand heading out to the beach, you could tell that a lot of thought went into this race.

The net of it all is that you now have a "streaker". As long as you put this race on, I will be a participant. In addition, you have gained a supporter in your fight against breast cancer. I was truly moved by this experience.

Thank you so much. I'll say a prayer for you and others who fight for the cure.

John Miles

>>>>

I wanted to thank Donna, Jeff, all the race organizers and volunteers for an amazing experience! I have never run a race before, and even though I was slower than I wanted to be, I had an amazing time and just enjoyed it so much. I will definitely be back next year. Also, I don't know how to thank them, but please know that all the folks on the streets through Jax Beach were just AMAZING! They kept me so motivated even though I felt like I was moving like a snail - the cheer, the signs, the water bottles, the snacks, the bands, the hoses - it was all so amazing. They made such a huge difference for me - I only wish there were some way for me to convey my thanks to each and every one of them!

Thank you again - Team Thomas will definitely be back next year!

Meghan Klingel

Annapolis, MD

>>>>

There were many highlights for me but my favorites were running on the Intercoastal Bridge (with the local News helicopter hovering above us no less!) and on the beautiful white sandy Jacksonville Beach. The supporters and crowds, many dressed in pink, were great too.

I look forward to running your Marathon again next year and to meeting you in person.

Sleepless, but very content, in Seattle, Thomas

>>>>

I just wanted to say THANK YOU for putting on such a wonderful marathon!

It was so awesome. From the crowd support, the beautiful course, meeting you and running with you for a minute along the course, the plentiful water/powerade/and gu stops! It was just great! And the amount of money raised for such a great cause was remarkable! Thank you for making it such a wonderful event. We plan to come back next year as well!

Jodi Green

> > > >

The organization was perfect from a to z from registration, busses, wc, water station, incredibly beautiful course and the support . . . wow . . .

amazing! I've posted a blog on my participation but being from Montreal, Canada it is in French . . . but here's the link anyway . . .

Congrats!!!!

Both my partner and I travelled from Vancouver Island British Columbia

Canada to run this race, and we have only recently returned home. May I say on behalf of us both what an incredible experience this was...anyone taking part must have genuinely thought this event had been honed and improved over many years, a great testament to the organisers, army of volunteers, and runners. Coming from the cold North, the heat was a struggle for us both, but the enthusiasm on the course was infectious, it certainly helped push me along.

I have always considered my hometown as the friendliest place in Canada, well, Jacksonville must certainly be the friendliest place in the U.S.

I (like so many) have lost friends and relatives to cancer, and feel your race is one of the most positive and poignant reminders that no one is alone in their fight. As a male runner I was also pleased to see three young ladies wearing T-shirts with "men get it too" on their backs.

We have already begun organising our winter "warm weather" run around your next 26.2 with Donna.

Once more we thank you from the depths of our being.

Chris Morrison (bib #4666) & Jackie Sharp (bib #4667)

> > > >

I close my computer and look up at the clock. It's 11:51 p.m. I've been reading for more than two and a half hours.

Where did the time go?

So much for getting to bed early and I'm still wide awake.

I down my three pink pills.

Will be so glad when I don't have to take these anymore.

I'm counting down the weeks. Four to go, and then my hands and feet can become human again. Hopefully my markers will be good. Edith will be content to follow me with scans and tests. Linda's doctor can give me some holistic things to focus on. I need a change of focus. Love letters from runners aside, with the race over, I've had way too much time to dwell on my swollen extremities and questionable prognosis.

Tim is asleep with his glasses now slightly askew on his face and his book resting on his chest. I look over to see what he's reading. *A History of God.* I gave it to him for Christmas. It's such a "Tim" book. He's a non-fiction guy and is especially enamored with anything that relates to God. I read almost exclusively fiction. I already get quite enough of the real world in my job. People do so many awful things to each other, and I get to be the bearer of all that bad news. Some days it's all I can do just to wipe it all out of my head.

I do have one exception to my fiction rule, a book that I started reading yesterday. My friend Dan Brown just sent it to me out of the blue. It's called *The Holy Longing: The Search for A Christian Spirituality* by Ronald Rolheiser. Dan was one of my literature teachers and the track coach at my Catholic high school, Bishop Kenny. He is not the author of The DaVinci Code. This Dan Brown always supervised our Lenten fast. Every year we would pepper him with the obligatory juvenile questions.

"Can we chew gum Coach Brown? Does that count as food?"

He always replied the same way, with the assurance that we could go out and eat steak if that was our desire. It was entirely up to us. Of course we never did. Coach Brown was one of those teachers you didn't want to disappoint. He wasn't just there for a paycheck. He was authentic. He listened. Kids can spot a phony a mile away.

I hadn't spoken with him since graduation beyond a quick hello at the Catholic Charities Ball. But we had reconnected just before my diagnosis. Dan was looking for help to raise money for a track at Bishop Snyder High School where he is now teaching. I wasn't much help at all, but it afforded us the chance to catch up.

As a teacher, Dan was always a great spiritual sounding board and I need to find a hook back into that part of my life. I'm going to Mass every Sunday, but I don't know how present I really am there. Even on those days when I can connect with the Holy Spirit at church, I've usually lost it by the time I hit the exit. There is just so much noise in my head. I have flashes of serenity, but that's all. I want some consistency. Tim has that. Sometimes I live on his faith, unable to sustain my own.

I have never shared any of this with Dan, but when I received the book it was almost as if he had read my mind.

I did find his inscription somewhat confusing.

Donna,

May the peace and grace of Our Lord and Mother, carry you lightly as you serve His people.

Dan Brown

Our Lord and Mother? Was he talking about Mary? I certainly have made no secret of my affection for the mother of Jesus. I have shared in previous writings what a comfort she has been through my most difficult times. I assumed as he often did in class, Dan was simply providing some intrigue for the subject matter. Before I knew it I'd spent the morning devouring the pages and then sent Dan a note of thanks.

From: Donna Deegan

Sent: Thursday, March 06, 2008 3:35 PM

To: Dan Brown

Subject: Thank you

Dan,

I started reading the book today. I have to share with you that your timing is an answer to prayers. Actually, an answer to prayers that have been hard to come by lately. For no particular reason, beyond the fact that I seem to go through periods of spiritual dryness I have had a difficult time praying lately. I have wrapped myself in the business of my life and what I hope I am doing for others and said basically "God this is going to have to do for now. I just can't go there." Not that I don't want to, more of a "Lord I believe, please help me in my disbelief" type of thing. Know what I mean? I am willing to be made willing, but right now I'm struggling to open myself.

Again, thank you so much. If you ever wonder if God is leading you to something, just know that you have given me a powerful tool and one that I look very much forward to using.

God bless,

Donna

When I told Tim about the book, he asked me to make sure I turned it over to him as soon as I was finished. Now, watching as he sleeps, I feel a wave of gratitude for the man he is. My rock. I hope I return to him half of the energy he gives to me.

Removing the glasses from his face, I brush his forehead with my lips and place his book on the nightstand.

Flip off his lamp, and flip on mine.

I lift the bookmark from the page I was reading in *The Holy Longing*. The section is called "Huddling in Fear and Loneliness." Page 116.

"Apostolic community is not had by joining with others who share our fears, and with them, barricading ourselves against what threatens us. It is had when, on the basis of something more powerful than our fears, we emerge from our locked rooms and begin to take down walls."

Those are the last words I remember reading. Five a.m. comes in a blink.

21 | *Turning the Page*

March 20, 2008

"What are you running from?"

Dr. Bridget Freeman is staring intently at me as she asks the question. Bridget is British. The lilt of her voice is melodic, comforting. Her teardrop shaped eyes peer out from behind wire rimmed glasses. Her reddish gray, shoulder length hair is half swept up in a clip, and looks as though it has no intention of conforming to any rules whatsoever.

Bridget is a hematologist oncologist. She began her practice treating children with cancer. She says it was her experience with those children that ultimately led her to a more integrative approach to medicine.

"I heard them tell the same stories over and over again," she told me.

"These children had absolutely nothing in common beyond the fact that they were terribly ill or near death. They talked to me about seeing angels. Their stories were strikingly similar."

Bridget said the accounts of what happened ranged from seeing deceased relatives, to out of body experiences.

"They would report seeing someone standing at the foot of their bed who they'd never known, never even seen a picture of. This person would say 'I'm so -in -so and I'm your uncle' or whatever the family relationship may be, and the children would go back and report this, much to the amazement of their parents," she said.

One child in the intensive care unit actually remembered watching from above as a family member walked out of her room and down the hall to get a Coke. When the person returned, the child remarked, "I'd like to have that Coke that's in your purse."

Some children even had religious experiences. She recalled one boy with Sickle Cell Anemia who was on a ventilator. When he finally recovered enough to talk, he told Bridget about what he'd done while he was away.

"I've had the most wonderful time. I got to spend the day with God. I could see my family sitting at the kitchen table at home, but I was so happy I didn't want to leave even to be with them. God told me it wasn't my time yet and that I needed to go back."

One girl had a room which faced the river and when Bridget came in she was staring out of the window, very distraught.

"I missed the ferry," she insisted.

"What ferry?" Bridget asked.

"Jesus came to get me and I didn't make it to the boat."

The girl died a short time later, moments after announcing Jesus had come back for her. "He's coming. Jesus is walking on the water toward me."

Over time Bridget became convinced that conventional western medicine was just the tip of the iceberg. She began studying eastern philosophies: the mind, body, spirit connection.

"What conventional doctors don't always see is that these three things are indivisible. You can't disconnect them. They are one and the same," she said.

Bridget now combines eastern and western philosophies to treat her adult patients. She has no quarrel with conventional medicine, in fact encourages her patients to complete their chemo therapy or other treatments, but she is certain that without the triad approach, sickness cannot be dissolved for good.

Her question for me comes after a rather lengthy discussion of my life in perpetual motion.

"Running from?" I repeat the question with no plans to answer it. Tim is sitting next to me but offers no help, preferring to let me answer for myself.

"What is it that is keeping your mind, body and spirit from harmony?"

"I'm not exactly sure," I say.

I look at Tim. "Should I share my crazy dream?"

"You shared it in your book, why not?"

I take a deep breath. I did write about this dream in my first book. I debated about it for days, and finally decided it was something I wanted to include. But it was a difficult story to tell.

"Go ahead if you like," Bridget says.

"Just days before I was diagnosed the first time back in 1999, I had a horrible nightmare. I was in a room that was completely white. I was bound and gagged. A madman was standing over me, carving a word into my stomach with a knife."

"That sounds very frightening."

"It was terrifying. The word he carved into my skin was 'trichot'. I didn't know it. Had never seen the word in my life. When I woke up, I remembered it so vividly that I immediately went to my dictionary to look it up. The closest word I could find was 'trichotomy'. The definition was the separation of mind, body and spirit."

"My, that's some dream," Bridget says. "I'm surprised that didn't lead you to seek out these answers sooner."

"I was under extreme, constant stress at the time. All self- imposed. Now that I look back on it, maybe the guy wasn't a madman at all. Maybe he was just trying to make me aware that I was killing myself."

"All stress is ultimately self- imposed," Bridget says. "And awareness is the first step to making yourself spiritually and physically healthy. You may be right about your so-called madman. Let's talk about awareness and energy for a moment."

Bridget pulls out a chart and places it on the table in front of me.

"This list shows life draining energy versus life giving energy," she explains.

At the top of the life giving energy is Enlightenment. It is followed closely by peace, joy and love. Each is given a point total. Anything below the level of neutral on this list is considered energy draining.

Shame, guilt, apathy, grief, and fear are the biggest energy robbers. Your basic staples of the human experience and I have been most decidedly human.

I am surprised to also see courage on this side of the ledger. Of course as a cancer patient, fear has become second nature to me. Courage, I always saw as a positive.

"Why courage?" I ask. "I don't understand why that would be negative."

"I wouldn't use that term. The goal is balance. Just remember everything that takes energy from you must be balanced with those things that give you energy. Having to muster courage doesn't charge your battery. It takes a lot of energy to be courageous doesn't it? If something requires courage, it means you must be fearful of it, you must be fighting," she says.

"Of course I'm fighting. I've had cancer three times."

"Perhaps that is partly why you've had cancer three times," she says, as confidently as if she had just told me that eating too much cake will make me fat. "If you are in a constant state of fight or flight, that's stress. You are placing your body under persistent stress if you are fearful."

The thought seems crazy to me. My whole mentality about cancer is tied up in "beating" the disease. That's the culture. We're in the fight of our lives. We're "battling." That's our identity. It makes us noble figures. Not victims, but stealthy warriors.

"How can I beat cancer without fighting it?"

"You don't beat it," she says matter-of-factly. "You stop fighting and start balancing."

Balance, Bridget explains, is the key to health in all ways.

She straightens the glasses on her face and leans forward.

"You never stop moving," she observes. "Stress isn't only mental it's physical and stress is what causes the inflammation response that enables illness. Between your work schedule, and your mom schedule, and your charities and your running, when do you have time to recover any of that lost energy? Your life has no balance."

"What am I supposed to do? Are you asking me to stop the world and get off? Go sit on a mountain top somewhere and meditate?"

"No, although some people do. You have to prioritize your life. Is there anything more important than getting healthy and staying that way? I have seen this scenario over and over again and I can tell you what will happen. You need to make choices. You can have some of all of those things you love to do, running included. Just balance the time you spend doing those things with some stillness. Learn to sit, quiet your mind and listen."

"Running is more than exercise for me. It's my escape. It's my peace."

"Escape isn't peace, Donna. What is it you are trying to escape?"

There is that question again.

I pause, not sure how to answer.

"The stress of the day I suppose, and it probably helps me to deal with the fear as well. I've always figured as long as I'm running I'm OK."

Bridget pulls another list from her folder and pushes it toward me.

At the very top of the page is the title of a book. *Love is Letting Go of Fear* by Gerald Jampolsky.

"This will explain how you need to change the very way you see your world if you are going to change your thoughts from fearful ones, to the loving ones that will help you. You will learn in Dr. Jampolsky's book that everything that is not love is fear. So when you talk about stress, you are talking about fear. You'll find the book very useful if you are willing to accept this premise."

"But stress is a part of life."

"It's all how you look at it, Donna. It's your choice. Wouldn't you like to give up the fear altogether?"

"Is that even possible?"

"Not only is it possible, it is necessary if you are going to achieve balance and bring your body back to perfect health. Fear doesn't serve you," Bridget says.

She goes on to suggest that I cut my running down to a few days a week for a while and for balance, in the off days, incorporate restorative yoga and meditation.

This is totally not my thing. I hate to sit still. If I'm moving I'm living. This is going to be incredibly hard.

"This is going to one of the most difficult things you've ever done," she says, reading my mind. "It takes discipline, but I am going to give you some tools to help you get started."

In addition to *Love is Letting Go of Fear*, Bridget has a list of meditation helpers. One is a CD series from Centerpointe Research. It starts with something called Awakening Prologue. The CDs are supposed to help my mind get into a meditative state more easily.

"There are other things," she continues. "You will need to give up wheat, specifically gluten, and all dairy products. Eighty percent of people are allergic in some form to those things, but they just don't know it. We are trying to eliminate inflammation. Remember, we want to take as much stress off of the body as possible."

My eyes are already halfway down the list. She wants me to see a dietician who can help me retool my diet. She wants me to travel to Orlando to see an acupuncturist named Dr. Zhi Huo, who has reportedly had great success with cancer patients, and then there is a list of medical tests she wants to perform to gauge the state of my health as we move forward.

"This is quite a list," I say, relieved that there are some physical action items for me in addition to the meditation.

"It is. And everything on that list is important. But none of the dietary or treatment options compares to the power of your own mind. You need to understand this. It is in changing your thoughts, stilling your mind that you will change your life. Studies show that you can actually influence the inflammatory response in your body, with your mind. You must find harmony on the inside before anything you do on the outside will make a lasting difference. You need to make peace with all of this Donna, or the rest won't matter."

Busted again.

Make peace with the cancer. There's a concept. Make peace with the fear.

"It sounds like surrender to me," I say.

"It sounds like freedom to me," Bridget says.

Tim has been in listening mode through most of this. Bridget turns to him.

"So how is your health?"

"Tim never gets sick," I say, not allowing him to answer for himself.

"I wouldn't say never," he says. "I would say very rarely."

"The people in this world who are rarely ill, are those who are generally filled with unconditional love," she says.

"That's totally Tim," I say. "He is the most loving person I know and the least judgmental."

Tim squeezes my hand and I continue.

"He's not an adrenaline junkie like me. He runs every day, but he makes time every morning for prayer and quiet. All of this would come much more naturally to him than to me," I say.

"I do need that time every day," Tim says. "I get up an hour before the rest of the house, read my *Living Faith* and the Bible readings that go with it and just spend a few minutes meditating about them. It just seems to set the tone for the rest of my day."

"That's exactly what it does," says Bridget. "You are setting an intention for the day. Meditation settles your mind and projects peace out in front of you."

"I'm looking forward to learning more about it," Tim says. "But right now ladies, I have to excuse myself. I'm late for work."

He kisses me goodbye and gives Bridget a long hug.

"You're very fortunate," she tells me, as the door closes behind Tim. "To have a partner who will support you in this is enormously helpful. Many people are not only fighting a disease they are fighting a spouse who thinks this is all a waste of time."

"This is where Tim lives," I say. "I remember one time asking him why he was so sure there was a world beyond this one. He told me he was more certain of that world than this one. I remember just being astounded by that. I don't think he has a fearful bone in his body."

"Well then, let's get you there," she says.

Driving home, I turn over the thought in my head.

Freedom from fear.

When is the last time I really felt freedom from all of this? I don't even remember what that's like. When is the last time I went ten minutes without thinking about it, obsessing over it, grieving about it, worrying what comes next? So much stress. Can I really give that up? It's almost an addiction. It is an addiction.

I look up and I'm sitting in a parking space in front of my favorite

Atlantic Beach bookstore, The Bookmark.

I have been so lost in my thoughts that I barely remember driving here. The Bookmark is a small, cozy store that invites book junkies to linger for hours all tucked away in a world of our own choosing. The owner Rona Brinley is my source for the latest "must read" novels. Several times a year I go in and say "load me up, Rona. I need my fix." She always knows exactly what books I'll enjoy reading. Today though, I am on a mission. I head straight for the counter.

"Hi Donna," Rona says. "Looking for something new to read?"

I pull Bridget's notes from my purse and hand her the title.

"*Love is Letting Go of Fear.* Yes, I know it. Give me a minute."

Rona disappears into a smaller room and soon emerges with a slim vanilla paperback.

"Here you go," she says, handing me the book. "I have some great new novels in if you're interested."

"I'm actually sort of in a non-fiction place right now believe it or not," I say. "I have this and another book to finish, but I'll be back."

I hand Rona the money for the book and get back to my car.

The book's cover has an illustration of a ship with the word 'LOVE' in capital letters on the hull.

A smiling man standing at the back of the ship is letting a rope fly that was attached to a small dingy. The dingy says 'fear' in small letters and the implication is that the ship is sailing away leaving fear behind.

I would like to sail away from my fear.

But how?

My eyes light on a phrase in the book's introduction.

"Teach only love for that is what you are."

I turn the page.

22 | *E*n Fuego

March 22, 2008

"Tim, may I read something to you?"

This is at least the fifth time I have interrupted my husband as he tries to concentrate on his weather maps. In truth, this is how we tend to read. To each other. I cannot get enough of this book, *Love is Letting Go of Fear.* Its simple message somehow seems revolutionary to me. It is certainly not the way I am used to looking at the world.

"Sure," he says, removing his glasses and turning to face me.

"*Sometimes we put more value in predicting and controlling than in having peace of mind. At times, it feels more important for us to predict that we are going to be miserable the next moment, and then find pleasure in being right, than to have true happiness in the present moment. This can be looked upon as an insane way of trying to protect ourselves.*"

"Tim that is so me! Dr. Jampolsky talks about how we all have these old movies from the past playing in our heads. Instead of living right now, the only time that actually exists, we spend all of our time projecting our past fears into the future and, what do we create in front of us? More fear, more sickness, more unhappiness. I've been setting myself up. I create the worst possible scenario in my mind. So I'm bracing myself for something that hasn't even happened. I thought I was being responsible, but what if I'm just more comfortable somehow being disappointed than banking on something I'm afraid I won't get."

"I've certainly derailed myself plenty of times with those same kinds of movies, but I think that's human nature," Tim says.

"Well maybe, but the book suggests that it's just our ego playing tricks on us."

"Our ego?"

"I'm not talking humility or lack of it here, the book calls it our false self. You'll like this. It says our real nature is love. In fact there's a line I really like "Teach only love for that is what you are." The idea is that we are all made from love. Unconditional love, not the jealous, possessive kind, and that everything that isn't love is fear. To put it in our language, if God made us in his image and God is love, then so are we. So if someone seems angry or jealous, or they feel guilty, or they're very judgmental, they are really just afraid of something. Rejection, or loss of power, being abandoned, stuff like that."

"Well, you've always argued that when people do destructive things, they are usually just afraid of something."

"I know, that's probably why I like it. You know how I like to be right."

"Aren't you always right?"

"Of course, but seriously, think about how many of the awful things people do to each other are based on past perceptions? People become bitter, they hold grudges. That's why it all starts with letting go of the past. Once you realize you're only hurting yourself with that garbage, hopefully you want to let go of it."

"This seems a lot like the other book you are reading," Tim says. "You read something to me about letting the past rise and bless you. Remember that?"

"That's *The Holy Longing* and you're right. There are definitely some of the same themes. Rolheiser talks about a sort of daily death and resurrection in our lives. But we have to be willing to let go of the past in order to receive its blessing."

"It sounds like one book just takes a more religious approach than the other."

"Well, yes. Some would say that's a big "just" but to me they are saying a lot of the same things. Doctor Jampolsky bases all of his teachings on a text called *A Course In Miracles*. It's sort of a compilation from The Foundation for Inner Peace. Overall, his words are less religious that Ron Rolheiser's. In fact, while he refers to God in his introduction, I wouldn't say his book is really religious at all. It speaks to everyone. Rolheiser starts off by talking about a number of different religions and paths to God. He talks about the need for mysticism in the spiritual life too, but ultimately he is talking to Christians. Did I mention he is a Catholic Priest?"

"Yes, you did."

"Let me see if I can find the section in the book you're talking about."

I go to the pile of books next to my computer and pull out *The Holy Longing*. I thumb through until I find what I'm looking for. Most of my books have markings all over them. All of the passages that I find most significant. This one is underlined with a star.

"Here it is, page 148. '*Name your deaths, claim your births, grieve what you have lost and adjust to a new reality, do not cling to the old, let it ascend and give you its blessing, and finally accept the spirit of the life you are in fact living.'"*

"It's all a choice," I say. "We have free will. So for me this means, I could wallow in the fact that I have now had cancer three times. I could live angry or fearful about that, convince myself of the worst. I could ask why me? Or keep grieving for my life before that, or I can choose to accept it, find all the good that has come from it and live in the reality of that present goodness."

"I think you do that mostly, don't you?"

"I think that is my public face, yes. And I do my best to keep moving forward, and to be positive, but that's not the same thing as letting go of the fear and allowing my past to be just that. If I truly believed the past had no power over me and I really lived in the present moment, I wouldn't be so afraid every time I walk into the Mayo Clinic, now would I? And that fear just translates to stress, which causes more illness. It's a vicious cycle. You've heard people say whatever you give your thoughts to is what gets bigger in your life. I need to focus my thoughts on love, and give the scary movies in my head a break."

"Wouldn't you say the type of love Dr. Jampolsky is talking about is simply the Holy Spirit?"

"To us, yes. Imagine if we could always feel the Holy Spirit in our lives. If we can really find a way to live in the flow of that love every day, what can we possibly have to fear?"

"Well, that's the challenge isn't it? If we could do that, this would be heaven."

"Exactly. Doesn't Jesus say the kingdom of God is within us? Don't we have to get there in our minds and hearts now? This book says our single function should be forgiveness. Doesn't that sound like Jesus? We're told not to judge others, only to forgive. If you were going to boil the main message we get from Jesus down to its essence what would it be?

"Love and forgiveness."

"Love and forgiveness," I repeat. "And Dr. Jampolsky says that this is the path to a goal of inner peace. Translated, forget the stress. But again, the kicker is we have free will. It's not going to appear magically on our doorstep. It takes practice and discipline. We have to quiet our minds and listen occasionally."

Tim smiles and looks at the floor. He is a listener from the word go. I'm the one who can't shut up. I am exceptionally good at talking. I can give God an earful, but how often do I just sit quietly, expectantly listening for a response? Not very.

"You know the Bible verse we always hear from Matthew, 'knock and the door shall be opened to you'? Well what I think I'm learning here is that it's not God who won't open the door, it's me. The love is always there, I've just been choosing fear instead."

For the first time in my life I am really aware of my own power. I can access God's love anytime I choose. It's a rush!

"It's sort of like that scene from *Finding Nemo*," I say.

"What?"

"You know when Nemo's dad, the Albert Brooks fish, is trying to find him, but in order to get to where his son is, he has to find his way to the East Australian Current? All he has to do is swim into it, and go with the flow."

To anyone else, I might sound like a raving lunatic. Fortunately I am swimming in familiar waters with my husband.

"I like that analogy. It's just that it's a big ocean with a lot of distractions."

"But that is why you start your day with your Bible readings and your *Living Faith* right? Then you meditate on what you've read. Like Bridget said, you've been setting the intention for your day, and how it will go, for years. You already live so much of this, Tim. We believe the same things. The only difference is I believe them mostly out of fear for what will happen if I don't, and you believe them because you believe in love."

"You're giving me a lot of credit here. I'm not a Saint. I struggle like everyone else."

"But not with this question. You've told me that. You don't worry about what's next after all this, because you believe in God's love. By the way, if you believe Rolheiser's definition, you may be a Saint. He has a great passage about what motivates us and why that's so important."

I go back to *The Holy Longing* and turn to another well marked section, page 66 and read.

" *To be a Saint is to be fueled by gratitude, nothing more, nothing less… We can will and do the right thing for the wrong reason… I can do all kinds of good things out of anger, guilt, grandiosity, or self-interest. Moreover, like the older brother of the prodigal son, I can be scrupulously faithful for years and years, but with a bitter heart. Sanctity is as much about having a mellow heart, as it is about believing and doing the right things. As much about proper energy as about truth."*

I close the book and look into Tim's eyes, now moist blue pools of emotion.

"My love, you have a mellow heart if there ever was one. For me, it's like I am seeing the world through new eyes. You know how I always love to wear those Oakley's with the pink lenses because they make everything look so much rosier? Well, what if by doing that, it becomes my reality? What if we all wore those glasses when we looked at each other? If that's all we saw, wouldn't that be our reality? Then we might be happier, and in turn, nicer to each other, and maybe one day we'd say, 'Wow we're all on this little marble together?' We're not separate, we're the same. And so by changing the way we see our reality, wouldn't we be eventually changing reality itself? I know it doesn't sound like me but it feels like the truth. Do you know what I mean?"

"Man, you are en fuego," he says. "On fire. I love it. And yes, I do know what you mean. It's wild how the truth can be standing there with you the whole time and you just don't see it. But once you recognize it . . ."

"En fuego," I say. "But it still requires action on my part. Just knowing won't get me where I need to be."

"And that's where the meditation comes in," Tim says.

"Yes, I have some CDs that will have me meditating for at least an hour a day, and also Dr. Jampolsky has a list of exercises here. It's basically a 12 step program for fear addicts. Every day I meditate on one of the steps. I read it in the morning, carry it with me during the day and internalize it. I apply it to everything that happens each day.

"Like what."

"Well, I'm really just getting to those. I did the first one yesterday. All That I Give Is Given To Myself. It means what I put out there comes back to me. If I only give what I want to receive, I will give only love. Not always easy when you are dealing with people who don't seem particularly lovable," I say.

"You're looking at me," Tim says.

"Present company excluded. Really, though it did make a big difference in my day. Just something as simple as traffic. A guy cut me off yesterday, and then he gave me the finger. My first instinct was like, what right does this guy have to be mad at me? He's the one at fault. But I remembered my intention for the day and I thought, 'OK what is this guy dealing with? Is he in a rush because his wife is in the hospital? Did he get fired today?' As soon as I gave him the benefit of the doubt, I felt better. It made me feel peaceful. I only hurt myself by being stressed out and upset. It's baby steps, but it helps."

"So what are you working on today?"

"Forgiveness is the Key to Happiness."

"Do you think…"

"Yes, I'll give you this one when I'm done too," I say. "In fact I'll order one for you from Rona at The Bookmark."

"Now will you stop interrupting my reading and go study your weather maps, geez," I say.

I pick up the phone and call Rona Brinley.

"Hey Rona, I need to order a book. In fact I need to order 10."

"Ten?"

"Yes, it's that book I got a couple of days ago. *Love is Letting Go of Fear.*"

"What, are you teaching a class?"

"Sort of. Can you get it for me?"

"Ordered and on the way," she says.

23 | To Bear

April 6, 2008

"This song always makes me think of Mary Pat," I whisper.

Tim nods and continues to sing.

We are at the 10 o'clock Mass at St. Paul's Catholic Church in our regular spot about three quarters to the front on the right side. The communion song is "How Great Thou Art." Tim's sister loves it because it always makes her think of their father.

"My burden gladly bearing," the song continues.

I feel a catch in my throat and swallow hard. Tim notices I've stopped singing and pats my hand. I've been so emotional in Mass lately and it makes me self-conscious. Even as I wipe the corners of my eyes I feel the warm drops escape down my cheeks. I'm not sad. Quite the contrary. I'm just fully present in the moment and its overwhelming.

"Mary cries when she hears that song too," I say, as we walk out of the church.

"You don't have to defend yourself, Donna. I think it's awesome that you're feeling the spirit like you are. It's nothing to be ashamed of."

"I'm just so," I pause to try to figure out just exactly what I am. "I'm so grateful," I finally say. "And so happy."

"Don't say it like it's a crime, darlin'," Tim says. "God wants you to be happy."

My thoughts go to Father Greg, my priest friend.

"God wants you to be happy." How many times has he said that to me? I have had so much trouble believing it.

"I'm going to give Father Greg a call today," I say, as we get into the car.

"Good, what made you think of that?"

"Oh all this just seems like something I should be discussing with him."

"Looking for permission to feel good?"

Am I? All of these books I've been reading. They aren't exactly right out of the catechism. Not as much guilt.

I color inside the lines. Not that I haven't let the crayon slip a few times. Sometimes I've colored clear off the page. I just don't put much into my head that could mess with my belief system. If I read something that doesn't correspond with my way of being, something that takes me outside my comfort zone, it scares me a little. All of these feelings, as wonderful as they are, still occasionally mess with that part of me that says 'Wait a minute! You don't deserve to feel this good.' I'm constantly checking myself.

"I don't think I'm looking for permission. I sent him a copy of *The Holy Longing* and I want to see if he's read it. He's had a rough time lately too. Both of his parents have been very ill, and you know he is the only person around to care for them. He's been trying to take care of them 24/7 and run the parish at Holy Family at the same time. I just want to check in on him."

Back at home I dial his number. He picks up almost immediately.

"Howdy kiddo, how's life?"

"I'm doing great, Padre. Three more days to go and hopefully I'm done with the chemo. I'm wondering how you're doing? You've certainly had your share lately."

"Well, it's been a difficult year. Mom and dad aren't doing well at all. You know the old saying though, God never gives you more than you can handle. Some days I let him know he has a little too much faith in me, but overall life is good."

"Well, you sound good. You always do though. Hey, have you had a chance to read that book I sent you?"

"Not yet. You seem pretty jazzed about it, though. I'm looking forward to getting to it."

"There's another one I want you to read when you're finished with that."

"Another reading assignment? You're on a roll these days."

"You know, I think I am on sort of a spiritual roll right now. You know how you always say God wants us to be happy? I've always watched you and wondered how in the world you seem to maintain a sense of joy no matter what your circumstances. I think I'm finally starting to get it."

"You know the secret, Donna? I wake up every morning and before I ever get out of bed, before I can ever give myself a chance to complain about anything, I start making a list of things I'm thankful for. I take the time to thank God for each and every thing in my life that I'm grateful for and do you know before I can get to the end of that list I truly can't think of one thing to complain about."

"That's exactly what it says in one of these books I'm reading. The idea is that gratitude brings more into your life. That by being grateful for what you have now, you create more things to be grateful for. Some of it is kind of out there, but it's really helped me to stay in the present, and refocus."

"There are plenty of places in the Bible that talk about gratitude. I've just had that practice for as long as I can remember, and it works for me."

"Well, if you can do that right now, with all you've been through, that says a lot."

"I think it's especially helpful now," he says. "But that's why I make it a habit. Since I do it every day at the same time it always puts me in a grateful place no matter what's going on. There's always something to be grateful for. Even if it's the fact that the sun came up. If you just look at what's in front of you right now, you can find something. You just have to choose to find it."

"A gratitude list every day. I'm on it," I say.

"I promise you, it works."

"I believe you. Let's have dinner soon, OK? It's been too long since we've caught up."

"Let's do it. Email me some times that work for you and the three of us can meet during your break one night."

"Will do. And read that book. I want to know what you think."

"You're very bossy, you know. You've been like that since you were a teenager."

"Well somebody's got to keep you in line, Padre."

"Tell Tim, 'Hi.' I'll look for those dates."

We hang up and I go to look at my calendar for possible dinner dates.

As I look, I'm singing to myself.

"…many are the blessings he bears to those who trust in his ways."

Tim walks into the room with his surfboard.

"Another song from Mass?"

"Father Greg says, 'Hi,'" I say. "And yeah, I've got this one stuck in my head."

"Well it's better than something like my 'My Sherona.' That's the one that usually gets stuck in my head."

"Oh, that is bad," I say. "You know what just occurred to me?"

"That you secretly love 'My Sherona?'"

"No. In the two songs we sang today, the word "bear", it means two very different things. In 'How Great Thou Art', "Our burden gladly bearing", to bear means to shoulder or to carry. In the other song, I think it's called Glory and Praise to Our God, to bear means to bring forth or create."

"OK professor, so?"

"So I just think it's interesting, that's all. Sometimes we have to bear something in order to bear something."

"That's a good one to ponder while I paddle," he says.

And he's off to his chapel in the sea.

24 | _Love_ Letters

April 21, 2008

Dr. Jampolsky,

I know you must receive millions of letters, but I am hoping you never tire of hearing how you have changed lives for the better. Your book, _Love is Letting Go of Fear_, was recommended to me by a holistic doctor I sought out to help me balance my life as I dealt with a third bout with breast cancer. I am a very public figure in my town and have had tremendous community support for my healing. I thought I understood the meaning of gratitude and love but the truth is, I was only letting others carry me for a while, never really healing from the inside.

I would invariably retreat back to my world where I was just waiting for the next bad thing to happen. I could create brilliant drama in my mind. All of it, I thought, simply preparing myself for whatever might come. So I knew immediately when I read your book that I had the ability to create quite the movie in my head and that all I would need to do was change the content. I know your program is not religious but I want you to know that as a devout Catholic, I would go to Mass every Sunday, pray that God would light me on fire with the Holy Spirit (very sincerely I thought) and by the time I would hit the steps on the way out, I was already derailing myself.

I bought your book looking for a way to heal my breast cancer. What I have received from it is a sea change in life. It sounds so simple and yet I never got it. I am living this moment in all of its beauty. The love (God for me) is right there all the time. All I have to do is see it in myself and others. I have learned this in countless quotes from the Bible, but I never really learned it with my heart until I read your book. I never felt it. Now whether I am in Mass, in the grocery store, at work, you name it, I feel I have the Holy Spirit with me. This may make you laugh, but I have bought the local bookstores out of every copy of your book (and then ordered more). I want EVERYONE I love to read it and these days that is becoming quite a list. I don't know if you still travel a great deal, but if you would ever be interested in coming to Florida, I would love to have you here to speak.

I have a Foundation that pays for the critical needs of breast cancer patients who need financial assistance. We run a marathon, actually just had our inaugural in February in which we raise money for that purpose and for breast cancer research. This includes a medical symposium, speakers at our race expo etc. If this is something that might interest you, I would be honored if you would consider it.

Truly this letter is just meant as a THANK YOU THANK YOU THANK YOU from the bottom of my heart.

```
Your mantra greets me every morning on my fridge.
Teach only love.  For that is what you are.
Gratefully,
Donna Deegan
```

I stare at the words I've written and finally send them on their way. Look up to see Tim standing next to the table.

"I'm sorry honey, I didn't see you there," I say.

"I guess not. You looked pretty intense."

"Oh, I finally sent a note to Jerry Jampolsky," I say. "I probably read it over a hundred times before I sent it. I feel sort of goofy now. He's probably not even going to read it. Can you imagine how many letters that man must get?"

"Well, my guess is he will read it, but either way, I think it's nice you let him know how much the book means to you. You really do seem much lighter these days."

"It's funny, you know, like I said in the note to Jerry, I got into this so focused on curing myself, but it's become so much bigger than that. Sometimes you just don't realize how much weight you carry around. You build it one rock on top of the other for so long, but it's so gradual that you just don't think you're weighed down, until one day you take the rocks off and it's just, wow!"

"I think the cool thing is we've learned that it's easier to reach the rocks on each other's backs. I can lift the ones off of your shoulders and you can lift mine, and we're both lighter."

"I love the way you think. Every time I share that book with someone I feel lighter. Just before I sent the note to Jerry, I sent one to Donna Nelson. Remember her?"

"Sounds like I should."

"She is one of my Donnas from the race, and a friend of Dan and Lorraine Hardaway."

"Not snapping," he says.

"Dan and Lorraine won the trip to the race. Anyway they were the ones who first told me about Donna. They've even started a blog spot in her honor called "The Pink Bandanna.""

"I think I remember Dan and Lorraine," Tim says. "So how's Donna doing?"

"Well, she just registered for the 2009 race, so that's great. I met her at the start line back in February. She wasn't running. She was just about to start chemo and she was afraid to run. Now she's almost done but she's sort of struggling. You know how it is when the chemo's gone on too long and it's just tough to keep slogging through it? I was there a few weeks ago. I can totally relate. Anyway, I shared Jerry's book with her. I hope it helps."

From: Donna Nelson

Subject: Donna to Donna

Hi Donna:

Just a note to say hello and hope you're doing well. You remain in my prayers. I went to my oncologist today. I have 3 Taxol left and then the 33 radiation treatments. Then I'm going on Femara for I guess 5 years.

I'm writing because I have a question. Do you ever just get tired of it? Or want to throw your hands up? I stay so very strong every day, not only for me, but for my loved ones. But sometimes, you know it all seems to be too much. Am I wrong to feel that way? Am I being selfish because of all my "sisters" who aren't going to make it? I mean I think I'm doing really well recovery wise, so how dare I despair. I hope you know what I'm trying to say . . . I guess it's just one "of those days." BUT . . . women like you and Wendy Chioji are my beacons of hope. You all remind that there is life on the other side. God Bless you all.

Thanks for listening Donna.

Sincerely,

Donna Nelson

*   *   *

From: Donna Deegan

Donna,

Everybody has their days, including me. Believe me. Don't beat yourself up for that. But don't stay there either. I try to look at cancer this way . . . without it, I wouldn't know how precious every moment is, I wouldn't be so focused on making sure every minute with my loved ones is spent in love and not on things that don't matter. I really do my very best to live in THIS MOMENT. I just focus on what I'm grateful for and by the time I say thank you for all of those things each day it's hard to feel bad about anything else. I would like to recommend a book to you. It's called Love is Letting Go of Fear by Gerald Jampolsky. It's a small book and one you can carry with you when you need a boost. It really did

help me to completely change my outlook. I just think we can out
positive this stuff. I think that Pollyanna had something! Just
keep plugging and stay focused on what makes you happy.

You'll get through it!

Blessings,

Donna

*   *   *

April 22, 2008

"It's just wonderful the way you've grabbed onto this, Donna."

Bridget is checking my pulse as she talks. Her office is more like a small
home, with a big kitchen table where we sit and chat next to the examining
room. Running water can be heard from a fountain at the front, and the
sweet smell of incense rises from a tray in the foyer. The whole
environment says "peace."

"The incense reminds me of Mass," I say. "That's always been such a
comforting smell to me."

"And the meditation, your work here, it has brought you closer to all
of that."

"Yes, it has brought me much closer."

Bridget stops what she's doing and looks off as if she's remembering
something.

"It's so interesting to see the patients who really get it," she says,
returning her gaze to me.

"Some people, like you, are very religious and it strengthens their faith. Others aren't religious at all, but they feel the flame of it, just the same."

A contented look settles on her face.

"It's lovely really. You seem very different from the woman I met last month. I'm proud of you."

"Well, it's like Dr. Jampolsky says, the teacher is there when the student is ready. It's almost like being in love. The whole world just seems like a better place. Don't you feel that way?"

"I do most of the time," she says, tucking a wayward curl behind her ear. "Not always. Occasionally life happens and I have my days, but you will too. And when you do, don't be too hard on yourself. It's like anything else. It takes practice and even then some days you will be more successful than others."

"I gave that very advice to someone yesterday. Oh, and I wrote to Jerry."

"Jerry Jampolsky? That's wonderful. I bet he'll write you back."

"He already has actually. I got his email this morning. Can you believe that? Less than a day after I wrote to him. You can tell he lives what he preaches.

From: Jerry Jampolsky
Subject: Boundless love and blessings
Dear Donna
I just received your love filled letter. Thanks soooooooooooooo very much for your kind thoughts and boundless gratitude for the way you have put the principles to work in your life.
We have cut down our travels and speaking engagement so we are going to have to take a rain check on your kind invitation.

By the way we worked with Mother Teresa and
Missionaries of Charity for a number of years.
Sending you BOUNDLESS LOVE AND BLESSINGS
Jerry Jampolsky

25 | Paying it Forward

May 27, 2008

I'm nervous. Excited nervous, but still nervous. It's a warm day, in the upper 80s and the air is saturated. The powers that be decided to hold the news conference outdoors in the courtyard next to the Mayo cafeteria. It's a beautiful venue, with the clinic's campus in full bloom, but it's sticky. As I ascend the steps to the meeting area, chairs are set up in rows with a lectern at the front. I can see the men in their ties already starting to loosen them.

It's so weird, my dual life here at the clinic. Patient, now benefactor. It's almost dizzying switching from one role to the other. Sometimes I'm an invited guest, attending committee meetings and giving instructions on all matters marathon. Other times more of a reluctant resident, being told what line to stand in and which doctor to see.

This morning, I am the former. I'll be presenting the clinic with a larger than expected check from our inaugural race.

I unroll the paper in my hand. It's the schedule of events for the morning. It is already moist with the sweat of my hands.

Julie walks up with two huge checks in tow. "The money girl has arrived," she says. "I need your signature on these."

"Are we going to take them to the bank? Actually that would be fun wouldn't it? Walk in carrying this humongous check and say, I'd like to cash this please."

"Well, these would be nice checks to cash," Julie says.

She gives me a quick peek at the amounts. Our inaugural race raised $832,043 making it the largest single day fundraiser in our city's history. The amount is split 70/30 with Mayo receiving the lion's share for research.

"Why don't I just sign them when I present each check?" I say.

"That works. Do you think we could get started soon? I am dissolving into a puddle as we speak."

I glance at my watch. It's 11:02.

"Good call, we're already late anyway."

I step to the microphone.

"Good morning, everyone! Thank you so much for joining us today. I know it's a warm one, so I'd like to get started. Besides, I've got some money burning a hole in my pocket and if I don't give it up soon, I'm going to have to go shopping."

I look into the crowd, and Edith is glowing. Literally glowing, and not from sweat. She has with her some members of her research team and I get the feeling she is ready to herd them all into the building the minute she gets the check.

"This all started with an idea and a vision. Two short little women who had this crazy notion that they could change the world," I say, looking directly at Edith. "We never wavered in our commitment to this race. And the more we believed the more others around us believed. I want to first of all thank Edith Perez for bringing Mayo to the table. So many people said it could never be done. I see Dr. David Miller in the crowd. David ran the half marathon as a payback for his non-belief. Remember that Dr. Miller?"

A light blush settles over Dr. Miller's face.

"How could I forget," he shouts.

"David made a bet with us when we first came up with the plan. He said we'd never get Mayo on board. Why he would think that I'm sure I don't know because you folks are always so easy to deal with."

The crowd laughs. The sarcasm is lost on no one. Mayo is notorious for its unwillingness to partner with others. The Mayo brand is considered too valuable to risk tarnishing.

"He said, if we succeeded, he'd run the race. And to his credit, he did. He almost killed himself because he didn't train, but he finished. Congratulations Dr. Miller and to the wonderful staff at the Mayo medical tent who I am sure made Dr. Miller feel much better after he crossed the finish line."

There is scattered laughter and applause and I turn my focus to Jeff.

"I would also like to thank Jeff Galloway who is here with us from Atlanta today. Jeff gave us the clout we needed with runners around the country and the world. Everywhere his training programs were focused on 26.2 with Donna and it showed. Our Galloway trainers and pacers were second to none and received rave reviews after the race. Jeff was a believer from day one and I thank you for that," I say nodding his way. The leaders of our local Galloway training team Amanda Napolitano, and Chris Twiggs were tireless in their efforts to get hundreds of runners on our team ready for the race, and in addition, our Jacksonville runners raised $81,000 that was added on to the total for the Donna Foundation. Chris and Amanda would you stand up please?"

Chris and Amanda rise to cheers from a number of our loyal runners who've turned out for the news conference. Among them Miles and Lisa Powell who have been with us since day one. Miles is a group leader and our biggest cheerleader. The ladies from his office have made and raffled two gorgeous quilts for the cause. Lisa is our team mom. She holds all our keys and makes the most mouthwatering gumbo for us on long runs.

"Twenty six pounds of shrimp," she said proudly after the last batch, holding out her pruned fingers for me to see.

"Now, before we all melt out here, let me ask Donna Foundation Director Julie Terrazzano and our board of directors to come forward to receive this check… drum roll please for $306,477."

The crowd applauds and Julie steps to the mic.

"Julie ran the half marathon, this year," I say. "Another bet gone bad, huh Jules?"

I sign the big check and hand it over to Julie. We exchange a knowing smile. Julie and I have been friends since elementary school at San Jose Catholic. Her mother was a breast cancer survivor and we've been locked together for this cause since my first diagnosis. I practically badgered her into directing the Foundation when it first started. She worked for free until we could afford to pay her. Now neither of us can remember how we survived without philanthropy in our lives. It's like crack. Once you get a little, you can't wait for the next hit.

"Donna, thank you so much," Julie says, throwing a furtive look my way. "Thank you for making me more sore than I have ever been in my entire life."

"That will teach you to doubt me," I say, wagging my finger at her.

"True enough. As you know this money will go a long way toward helping women and men in our community who really need us. We invited some of our recipients to the race and they were so grateful."

The words catch in her throat. Julie gets to know these women in a far more personal way than I do. She is wholly invested in lightening their burdens.

"They are always so grateful for everything," she continues. "One of them was a woman who was taking three bus connections just to get to her chemotherapy appointments and having to haul her small children along with her. Her husband had left her when she was diagnosed. She had no transportation and no way to pay for child care. We were able to step in, get her a ride to her treatment, find her some daycare, and we got her back up to speed on her mortgage, which was more than a month behind. It is so nice to be able to lift some of the stress from these people during a time that is already so stressful. This is just one example of the more than 1500 women we have reached out to through the Donna Foundation. On their behalf, I say thank you."

The crowd applauds as Julie steps aside.

"Thank you Julie. Now I'd like to bring up Dr. Edith Perez to accept the check for Mayo Clinic."

Edith almost races to stand beside me.

"I always love to see people's faces when they realize what a jewel we have in this community," I say. "Right here in Jacksonville, Florida we have one of the top breast cancer researchers in the world. I would tell you to google her name only you might crash your computer with the volume of her accomplishments. When Edith and I cooked up the idea for this race, she was the main reason I knew we would be successful. This woman has the mind to help solve this puzzle. She has played an integral role in the greatest advances we have made in treating breast cancer in the past ten years. But beyond the mind, she has the heart. Edith has a love for her patients and her work like I have rarely seen in a physician. She believes we will get there, and she believes in every patient, and that is what we need. Not someone who says here is what I can't do, but someone who says I can, and I will. I am thrilled when I can tell our runners that their money goes right here, to her research. They don't have to wonder what their dollars fund. They go directly to this brilliant woman and her team. Edith, I am so pleased to present you with a check for $525,566 for your important work."

Edith makes a dramatic swooning motion as she looks at the amount. I hand over the check to loud applause from the Mayo team.

"I couldn't be more proud of what we have started here today," Edith says.

"I want to thank Donna for her vision and her energy, and I want to thank my wonderful family here at Mayo. I would like for the members of my research team who are with us today to stand up."

One by one the people who hold the future of this disease in their hands rise from their seats.

"We are entering a time in which a one size fits all approach to breast cancer is becoming a thing of the past," she says.

Edith begins to explain the genomics project that the funds from the marathon will support.

"In the future we will be able to treat each woman specific to her own DNA," Edith explains. "The concept is to establish a formal program to test patient's tumors for molecular abnormalities to guide the selection of the potential best therapy for each patient. We have already set up our systems for tumor collecting and banking, and have also started to develop the system for cell culture and molecular testing. This plan will be collated with our clinical trials program to help identify new targets and bring new agents into the clinic. These studies will be led here in Jacksonville. Members of this research team will also be located across our three Mayo Clinic campuses with collaborators from other institutions. We are on the right path, and with continued support, we will set up this laudable project, with the goal to get us closer, one step at a time, to enhance the cure rate for this disease. With your support we can do this."

As she is talking I think about my own DNA and the research that is being done on the tumor cells that were taken from my body. I think back to the night of my surgery, to Tim's excitement over the fact that my tissue was the first to be banked for this new project. The warmth of the day loses its grasp on me and the thought of actually being a part of the cure gives me chills.

26 | Ohmmmost

I push the button on my CD player and take my place on the living room floor. A tone sounds.

"Please take a moment of silence to prepare yourself for this guided practice in meditation."

The soothing voice of the man Bridget calls my guru is wafting through the air of my living room. I am sitting on a big area rug, yoga style, spine erect, eyes closed. I am supposed to clear my mind of all thoughts as I listen to the instructor. This is a new exercise for me. My other meditation recordings simply involve listening to sounds and letting my mind float wherever it wants to go.

"Begin this practice by becoming aware of the breathing process," the voice says. "Simply monitor how your body is breathing for at least five exhalations and inhalations. Do not be anxious over the counting of the breath… allow the breath to be natural."

My mind is in no mood to cooperate.

What? Of course I'm anxious over the counting of the breath. How is this natural? Shhh you're not supposed to think, just listen.

"When the breath changes, be aware of the change and how the body wants to breathe . . ."

I don't breathe like this! Maybe I should slow down. Oh wait, I'm not supposed to force it. OK, not thinking, just breathing.

"Slowly without interrupting the awareness of your breath, bring some attention to the body and make adjustments to bring the body upright . . ."

It's hard to sit this straight. I think my foot is falling asleep.

"Gently become aware of the flow of air through your nostrils… feel the warm exhalation. Feel the cool inhalation . . ."

What's that smell? Did I forget to turn off the oven?

WILL you STOP thinking!

"Ultimately become aware of the silent space between your eardrums . . ."

What silent space?

"Remain absolutely still and observe the stillness. Any inclination toward the slightest movement simply be aware . . . Do not yield. Remain still."

My back itches. If I could just move for a second, I could reach it.

NO! You are not supposed to move, just be still.

But my back itches!

"Abandon all thoughts of the body and be aware of the stillness…"

This is torture! I have to move. I have things to do.

"If you wish, you may break the practice at this time, or you may continue as long as you can remain absolutely still."

That's it. I'm outta here.

I hop up, and turn off the CD player. I feel like a complete failure at this. This beginner's session only lasts a few minutes, but it feels like an hour to me.

How do I completely turn off my thoughts? I'm a mess!

I go to the kitchen and begin taking out the vegetables I'll use to make my green juice. This is part of my new no gluten, no dairy, vegetable rich diet. I'm actually really enjoying this. I have been taking allergy medicine my entire adult life, and since changing my diet, not one pill.

My son Drew walks into the room.

"Hey Mom, can you make me some lunch?"

"Sure buddy, what do you want?"

"Do we have any real food?"

"If by real food you mean food that is not organic, no we don't. What do you have against organic food? It just means there are no pesticides or hormones. It's more natural. Why is that bad?"

"I like junk, Mom. I'm a kid. Can you just take me to a drive-thru?"

"Come on Drew-dog," I say. "What if I make you a little cup of my green juice?"

"That stuff is gross."

"Gross? Come on it's good for you." I say, shaking the dark green leaves his way.

"What's in that stuff anyway?"

"Oh, let's see here," I say. "We've got black kale, some broccoli, cucumber and then ginger to give it a little zip."

"And what's all that going to do for you Mom? Make you live an extra 15 minutes?"

"Hey, a lot can happen in 15 minutes. I can watch you strike out a batter, or walk across the stage at your graduation, or get married."

"Mom, you can't get married in 15 minutes."

"Some people do. But you get the point."

"No, I don't. Are you going to take me to get food or what?"

"You're lucky I love you, Andrew."

Drew gives me his patented smile and I go off to search for my keys.

"Let's go there burger boy. I don't have all day," I say.

We climb into my car and Drew immediately turns on the radio. The voice that comes out is actually from another CD that I've been listening to. I've been learning about setting an intention or a mantra for my day, but this particular track is about visualization.

"Visualization is a key to bringing your intention into being . . ."

"Mom, please don't tell me you believe this crap," he says.

"You don't?"

"Of course not."

"Well, that's interesting, because I would think as a baseball player you would understand how important visualization is to your success."

"So, you think if I just visualize myself as a great player, that's going to make me one?"

"I think if you talk with any successful athlete, he or she would tell you that visualizing themselves scoring the point, or hitting the ball, or running the race, absolutely affects their ability to perform at crunch time. Drew 99 percent of sports is in your head."

"No mom, it's in my arm. If I don't pitch well, I don't play."

"So you don't think visualizing your perfect pitching motion, seeing yourself getting strikes, you don't think that would help."

"Not at all."

"Well, you're wrong."

"Great come back, Mom"

"I'm just telling you, Drew, that's what I do when I run a race. I see myself running strong, I see myself crossing the finish line. I believe in that picture and that's what gets me to the finish."

"Whatever you say, mom. Can I turn on the radio?"

"Sure. I'm not going to force this stuff on you Drew, but if you ask your coaches, if you ask some of the athletes you respect, I promise you, they will tell you the same thing. Almost all of your success or lack of it is in your mind."

"So how does this help you, Mom? You think you don't have cancer so you don't have cancer?"

"Well, not exactly. There's more to it than that. But there are certainly a number of studies that show visualization can improve the outcomes of people with cancer. If I see myself in perfect health, and really believe that, I think my body responds. It's not the whole answer, but it's a piece of it."

"Positive thinking," he says.

"No, not just positive thinking. If I visualize it, I am actually seeing the outcome in my mind. I'm excited about being healthy, I'm grateful for it."

"You're grateful for something you don't have yet," he says. "That doesn't make sense."

"Well, first of all, all of my scans since my surgery and chemo have shown that I'm cancer free, so I would argue that I do have it, and I'm just working on staying that way. But let's say that wasn't the case. I'd tell you I am laying the groundwork to have it, by sending my thoughts ahead of me. Does that make sense?"

"Not at all."

"I know it's sort of a tough concept to grasp, especially for a 13 year old. You guys are immortal. But I believe it."

Drew doesn't argue anymore, he just flips the radio dial to his favorite rap station and after a few minutes I find myself longing for the silence I was so anxious to escape.

My phone rings.

"Hey Drew, turn that down for a minute. I've got a call."

He turns the radio off and I hit the answer button on my cell.

"Hello?"

"Donna, it's Linda White."

In addition to being my Bridget Freeman connection, Linda is teaching me restorative yoga. Also, her father-in law John has been seeing the acupuncture physician Bridget recommended for me. John had prostate cancer, and swears this Dr. Huo cured him. John drives three times a week to Orlando for treatments. He wants me to go too, but I'm not about to make that trip with all I have going on. I-4 traffic is not going to do anything to reduce my stress.

"Hey Linda, what's up?"

"Donna, John just called me and he's so excited. Apparently Dr. Huo is coming to Jacksonville."

"Coming as in visiting, or moving?"

"From what I understand he is going to come to the Wellness Center twice a week from now on. He's had so many patients driving to Orlando to see him that he finally agreed to come here. John just feels so strongly that you two should meet."

"I'm all for it. I think you know I am already seeing Ingram Caswell for acupuncture. I'm very comfortable with her and I think she's really helped me to get to a more peaceful place, but I'd love to see what is so special about this guy."

"Can you write down a phone number?"

"No, I'm driving. Why don't you just call back and leave it on my cell phone."

"OK, will do. If you just call The Wellness Center, they'll set you up with an appointment."

"I'll call. Bye, Linda, thanks."

I hang up, and turn to Drew. We are at the order station at the drive through.

"Know what you want?"

"A number five."

"Number five please, water to drink," I say into the screen in front of me.

"I want Coke," Drew says.

"Don't push me, son. Water is the least you can do for me here."

We drive up to wait for the food.

"Are you letting people stick you with needles?"

"Yes, I've been doing that for a few weeks, but there's a new doctor I'm going to see. He supposedly is very successful with cancer patients, so I'm going to check him out."

"You couldn't pay me enough to have someone stick needles in my body."

"They don't hurt. They're so thin, you can't even feel them going in."

"I know, Mom, you just visualize them not hurting and magically they don't hurt."

"You are a jerk, you know that, don't you?"

"I know, I'm lucky you love me," he says laughing.

"Exactly."

27 | *Happy* Huo

Want It

Expect It

Receive It

The phrase is framed in black and white, and hanging on the wall across from where I'm sitting. It makes me smile. Not exactly the type of thing I'm used to seeing in a doctor's office. Unless it's Bridget's office, which it is not.

I think back to my first conversations with the integrative medicine doctor who has now become a source for so much of my daily routine.

"Your thoughts are a big part of your healing process, Donna. If you want perfect health, think of yourself in those terms. Internalize it, believe it, and you will draw it to you," Bridget told me.

"No offense, Bridget, but this sounds like a bunch of spacey nonsense to me," I said.

"Roll your eyes if you want to, Donna, but you need to get your arms around this. Your thoughts are powerful. They become the things in your life."

"So if I can heal myself with my mind, why do I need medicine?"

"We treat mind, body, and spirit, Donna, all three have value. Whenever someone comes in here and says 'I don't want to take my chemo, I just want to meditate', I tell them to reconsider, to use every tool they have. Unfortunately so many western doctors don't see that on the flip side. You are fortunate in that doctors were able to remove your cancer. Now you are in a wonderful position to balance your body, to make it work as it should. That begins and ends with your thoughts."

That conversation took place only three months ago. It seems a lifetime away now.

Closing my eyes, I picture myself in perfect health. White light fills every cell of my body. From the tip of my toes to the top of my head, it sweeps through me, carrying with it all stress, all worry, all anxiety, all disease. I envision all of it streaming out of me, replaced by love and happiness and peace. I take a deep breath, and then another, suspending my thoughts altogether and simply focusing on the rhythm of my breathing. I'm meditating daily now, and this process is beginning to come more naturally to me. The chattering voices in my brain that want to distract me are more subdued.

Sitting on a cot at the Wellness Center waiting to see Dr. Huo, I could be anywhere. I am startled by a knock on the door. It takes me a moment to recognize my surroundings.

A nurse pokes her head inside the room.

"Hi, I'm Nina. You have a 10 o'clock appointment with Dr. Huo?"

"Hi Nina, yes I do, but the ladies out front tell me he's not here yet."

"He's running a little late, but believe me, you'll know when he's here," she says cheerfully.

She disappears into the hallway and a few moments later I hear the most uproarious laughter.

"HA HA HA HA HA".

Loud and clear and crisp. Not a jumble of sounds like most laughter, but HA HA HA HA HA. It's as if someone scripted the words and said "say them just like this and don't skimp on the volume". The most joyful sound! And totally contagious. Others begin to laugh too and so do I. I'm sitting in a room by myself, giggling like a child.

There is muffled conversation and then the laughter starts again. The door opens and in walks the happiest looking man I have ever seen in my life. His skin is tanned, his hair is jet black and swept back off his face. His dark eyes seem to throw off sparks. And that smile.

"Donna, meet Dr. Huo," says Nina.

"Well, I think I already have. I've been laughing with him for ten minutes."

"I am a happy guy. Call me Happy Huo," he says with his thick Chinese accent. And with that he laughs again.

"It's so wonderful having him around," says Nina. "He just lights up the whole place."

"Why would I not be happy?" he says as if it's the most natural state in the world.

"Doctor Huo, it's a pleasure to finally meet you. John White has told me so much about you," I say.

"Yes, John White. He had prostate cancer. Now, all better. I tell him he doesn't need treatment anymore but he keeps coming back. Must like my personality," he says.

"I think he worries what will happen if he stops coming," I say.

"Yes, but no need to worry. I tell him this, but he doesn't believe it."

"Well now he doesn't have far to go anymore," I say. "Why drive all the way to Jacksonville? It sounds like you have a thriving practice in Orlando."

"Global warming," he says, completely dead pan.

"What?"

"Twenty-five cars drive from Jacksonville every week to Orlando to see Dr. Huo. Bad for global warming. Now Dr. Huo drives to Jacksonville. Only one car. Good for global warming," he says.

"So you decided to come here to save the planet."

"I want to help the clinic too. Nice people. Very nice. They ask me to come. And when I see people getting better," he says putting his hands over his heart, "it makes me very happy."

And I can see that it truly does.

"Well, I know John is very happy too," I say.

"John has told me about you too. You had breast cancer," he says.

"Yes, three times."

"Tell me."

I go into my whole long medical history.

"So I'm now cancer free, and I'm here because I want to stay that way. All of my scans are good, but my marker numbers are a little higher than I'd like. It would be good to see them come down."

"They will come down," he says with a deep bow of his head. "Let me show you something."

He leaves the room and comes back with a video player and a briefcase. He plugs the player in the wall and opens the case to reveal literally dozens of tapes. Each is labeled in Chinese.

"I want you to see these before I treat you. These are people who come to Dr. Huo for treatment."

"Oh, I don't need to see the testimonials," I say. "My doctor, Bridget Freeman, and John have told me you've had wonderful success with all kinds of ailments."

"I want you to see," he says.

I agree.

The first tape is a boy with cerebral palsy, the second, a man with uncontrollable shaking, and finally a woman with breast cancer. All were taped at the beginning, middle and end of their treatments. All claim to be cured by this Chinese physician.

"You don't have to watch all of them," he says popping the third tape out of the machine. "These people all come to me because they are told there is nothing else to do. No one can help. So I help."

He certainly doesn't lack in confidence. I remember John telling me that. Yet there is a definite humility in this man.

"How long ago did you treat the woman with breast cancer?" I ask.

"About four years ago," he says. "She came to me because she was pregnant. Her doctor told her she should not carry the baby. She didn't want that so she asked if I could help her. I treated her for three months. Now four years later she is very good. Has more children. Very happy."

"No chemo?"

"No, she was afraid for the baby."

"How do you feel about that?"

"Her decision, of course. I tell people chemo is good, too. Eastern and western medicine work best together. In China I am a medical doctor. I write prescriptions, give anesthesia. We don't have so many specialties in Chinese medicine like here. Here I am very limited. Just acupuncture. In China, we treat the whole body. My uncle performed the first ever case in the world of, (he makes a chopping motion with his hand) hand cut off, put back together."

He goes to his briefcase and pulls out a page from an International Who's Who.

"This is my uncle," he says, pointing to the words he has highlighted in yellow.

Chen Zhongwei, Chinese surgeon; succeeded in replanting the severed arm of a co-worker in Shanghai- the first operation of this kind in the world 1963.

"That's very impressive," I say. "Do you ever go back to China?"

"Next month, I go back. The government wants me to treat the Olympic Athletes," he says.

"What an honor."

"Yes, I am happy to go."

"Happy Huo," I say, which prompts another laugh.

"When you're finished with me, I want to be as happy as you, OK?"

"Why not happy?" he says his eyes widening as if this is astonishing news.

"I'm mostly joking. I still let myself worry every now and then, but I'm so much better than I was."

"Happiness is on the inside," he says.

"Yes, I get that. You're a good example," I say.

"We will get your Qi (pronounced chee) moving and you will feel better," he says.

"I know something about Qi. I've had acupuncture before. It's the body's vital energy right?"

"Yes. I have very strong Qi, so I have good health. Think of it like a car battery. You have a weak battery. I have a strong battery. With needles, I use my Qi, my strong battery, to charge yours. I make your immune system strong."

"So is all of Chinese medicine based on Qi?"

"There are ten principals of Chinese medicine," he explains.

He takes out a pen and pad and draws two columns down the middle of the page.

"Every principal has an opposite principal," he says, writing the opposites side by side.

Yin	Yang
Qi	Blood
Internal	External
Cold	Heat
Deficiency	Excess

"Everything is about balance. If there is too much of one, I must treat to balance with the other. Imbalance makes sickness."

"And you treat certain points in the body to bring balance," I say.

He nods.

"I treat with herbal medicines and with acupuncture. I will try to explain."

"Certain points on your body stimulate your immune system. This one is for the Qi."

He shows me a spot on my lower leg.

"This one is for the blood," he says, pointing to a place just above my knee.

"I also do something called 'five needle acupuncture' on the head. I teach seminars on this all over the world. There are five elements in traditional Chinese medicine in addition to the ten principals. They are wood, fire, earth, metal and water. Each element is connected with an organ in the body. We have the lung, heart, liver, spleen and kidney."

"But what if you are treating the breast?"

"I treat the lung," he says. "The lung is the point for breast cancer."

"I don't get it."

"You are used to thinking a different way," he says. "Each element is connected to an organ, and also a season like winter and to senses like taste, and emotions like joy and fear, and anger. Do you see?"

"Not really," I confess.

"For instance, if I treat the liver, I am not saying you have a physical problem there. When Qi is not moving freely through the liver, people can be angry. When you see someone in road rage, you know that is liver Qi stagnation. If I treat the lung, I may be treating sadness or grief. When someone has lost a friend or loved one and they are sad and they cannot release that sadness, this can lead to illness so we treat the point on the head associated with the lung."

"I can't tell you how many women I have talked with who got cancer weeks or months after going through a divorce or losing a spouse. Now I think I understand why."

"Yes."

"So to you the mind, body and spirit are the same."

"Now you got it," he says, flashing that brilliant smile.

"That is Chinese medicine. Of course they are the same. Can you separate one from the other? No. I cannot treat one without treating all."

"That makes sense to me," I say.

"No more questions?"

"I'm sure I will have a million, but I'm ready to get started if you are."

"Good."

Dr. Huo places two needles in my legs, two in my hands in the space between my thumb and forefinger, and five in my head. One in the middle, one slightly above each temple, and two in the back. I barely feel them going in.

"The back is for balance," he says, as he taps the last needle.

"That's the goal," I say. "Now what?"

"Now you rest," he says. "I'll come back every few minutes and manipulate the needles. You'll be here for about 45 minutes."

He walks out, flips off the light, and I am alone. I hear his laughter, as he floats from room to room visiting with other patients.

This guy could light an entire city with his energy. Such a different experience than being with Ingram. She is so peaceful, and when I leave her I am peaceful too. Here, I can almost feel my body humming with electricity.

Dr. Huo sweeps into the room and without a word uses one hand to turn each needle while the other hand hovers over it.

He looks like a magician.

He does this four more times, and then retracts the needles and dabs each spot with a cotton ball. Then he pulls several small packets out of his pocket. They are filled with what looks like dirt.

"You will take these for two weeks," he says. "Three on the first three days, then two for two days, then one for two days. Then you will start over."

I repeat his instructions.

"Like a wave," he says motioning with his hand. "Mix with warm water, but not too warm. Here, let me show you."

He takes one of the packets and comes back with two ounces of warm water in a cup.

"Mix and drink," he says.

"What is it?"

"Mucus powder."

"What does mucus have to do with cancer?"

"In Chinese medicine we believe too much mucus can help cancer to develop. The herbal powder dissolves the mucus."

I drop the powder in the water and down it. It's awful.

"Tastes like pond scum," I say.

"Next time I bring you Coke," he says. "Tastes much better. Will not help your numbers go down though."

"I love pond scum," I say. "Really, I do."

28 | *W*inner

September 5, 2008

It's Friday morning. Sitting on my balcony watching as the soft colors of dawn give way to a golden sunrise over the ocean. I close my eyes and listen to the sounds of morning. The waves roar in, crashing hard against the sand. The surf is bigger than normal. It's really the only sign that something is brewing in the tropics. We are now in the core of the Atlantic hurricane season. Hanna is out there somewhere and Tim is busy watching her. I have a funny feeling in the pit of my stomach. Not bad really, just unsettled.

I adjust my bathrobe and look over at Tim who is already poring over his weather models. He's been up since 5.

"Honey, Hanna's not going to bother us this weekend is she?"

"Nope, doesn't look like it."

"Amanda was wondering if we were going to have to cancel our Saturday run."

"I already spoke with her. She sent out her weekly training blast. We're going to run. But you should read it, Donna. It sounds like Dr. John isn't going to be with us much longer."

"We should probably try to get over to see him in the next day or so Tim," I say.

"OK. How about tomorrow after the run?"

"Good."

I come into the living room, closing the sliding glass door behind me and sit down at the table that also serves as the home for my laptop.

I log in to check my email and there on top is a message from Doug Alred. Doug has taken on a much larger role in our race preps this year and I get emails from him now almost daily. I'm looking for Amanda's blast, so for the moment I ignore it.

Here it is.

Hey Group Leaders!

I think Hanna is going to spare us this weekend, and we will be able to run as a group from One Ocean Saturday. Chris will be out of town, so I am leading the charge! Attached is the 8 mile course that is our typical beaches run that loops out to Ocean Walk, down to the end of Seminole (TWICE), through Selva Marina, around Selva Lakes, and back to One Ocean.

Getting Started: Miles and Lisa, can you guys handle the group this weekend without me? My Group Leader is out of town, so I need to take a group.

Water Placement: Following are proposed water placement assignments, please confirm and let me know if you need any support.

Start/Finish: Miles and Lisa?

Ocean Walk Pool: Mary Binkley?

Selva Lakes: Susan and Dennis?

Shelby's is providing food and beverage following the run, and we will have merchandise for sale as well. Please encourage your groups to go over to Shelby's after the run!

As most of you know, Dr. John is now in Hospice on Sunbeam Road. He is in Room 211. Several of us visited him yesterday, and he is in remarkably great spirits! His signed poster that we gave him at the Group Leader appreciation is sitting proudly over his television. The drugs are making him loopy, but because they are making him comfortable that's ok by me. I'm sure he would enjoy a visit from each of you. I am about to send a similar notice to the entire group, but wanted you guys to know first.

Amanda

I remember the last long talk I had with Dr. John. We had given him some special gifts at the group leader appreciation dinner and when it was over he needed a ride home. I was grateful for the time alone with him. Usually Dr. John is so concerned about making everyone laugh that I never really get a good idea of how he's doing. The 30 minute drive gave me a chance to go deeper. He was weak, but extremely talkative.

"I've had a great life, Donna," he told me. "I've had a lot of wonderful friendships. Done my share of races, hopefully helped a few people. And recently I did something I've always wanted to do. I spent some time in the seminary. If by some miracle I get to stay around a little longer that would be great, but I am really fine either way."

"Susan Mehrlust said similar words to me once. It was a peace I couldn't grasp."

"And now?"

"I'm getting there," I said, with a smile. And I meant it.

Now as I look at Amanda's update, I am anxious for a last conversation.

"Maybe we should go tonight," I say.

I scroll back up to my note from Doug, and any thoughts of a final goodbye are erased.

Just wanted to let you know that John TenBroeck passed away this morning. John served the Jacksonville running community for over 40 years. He will be greatly missed.

Doug

My head sinks into my hands.

"He's gone, Tim. I just got a note from Doug. Dr. John passed away this morning."

Tim sighs.

"God bless him. It's not going to be the same without him on Saturday mornings. We should come up with something special to do during the race this year."

"We will. I want to do something on the air too."

I pick up the phone and call Amanda. She knows.

"I can't stop crying," she says. "For so many years, he's been the heart of the program."

"He still is, Amanda. You're just going to have to find some corny jokes to tell on Saturday mornings in his memory. He'd like that. Do you have some good pictures of him? I want to put together a piece on the news today."

"I have some. I'll ping Dawn Hagel too. She probably has a ton. Not to mention some great stories. Have you ever heard the one about how Dr.

John got his name?"

"I haven't."

"Well, I'll let Dawn tell you. It's classic. He was the happiest when he was making people laugh."

At the station, I collect all of my best Dr. John moments from the Friday running journals that chronicle our weekly training. The journals run every week during my evening broadcasts so I have plenty to choose from.

My co-anchor Shannon Ogden sticks his head into the edit bay where I'm looking at tapes.

"Hey there, miss oney-one with the universe. What are you working on?"

I love that Shannon calls me this. You know that old commercial that gives you the cost of things… such and such ten dollars and so on, and then gets to the punch line and it says "priceless." Working with someone day in and day out who totally gets you . . . Priceless.

Like me, Shannon is a huge fan of journalism, but he has a broad life outside the box. He's a talented musician. At one point was a session drummer. Recently he bought a guitar and taught himself to play in two weeks. Not pick at it. Play. He's also been a professional stand-up comedian. A skill that comes in handy in this job. He knows more obscure facts about Russia than a human being should know. And he has an amazing knack for memorizing any Will Ferrell movie word for word. His favorite, of course, *Anchorman*. Shannon adores sarcasm at least as much as I do, but is totally down with my new found Ohmmmness.

"I'm putting together a tribute to Dr. John," I say. "You know our running coach that was sick? He died this morning, and I'm trying to pick out some favorite clips to show at 5:30."

"I'm sorry to hear that."

"You know what's bugging me though?"

"You? Bugged? That's not very oney-one-ish," he says, smiling.

"I'm trying to make you feel better about yourself," I tease.

"Think about it though Shannon, I just don't get why people always have to say so-in-so lost his or her battle with cancer. Like somehow they're losers. We celebrate survivors, but aren't we all just surviving life until we move on? I mean life is a terminal situation is it not? Why does everything have to be a battle or a fight? I don't like the terminology."

"I think you just came up with a good subject for your blog."

"You know what, I think you're right."

Tribute to John TenBroeck

Posted 9/5/2008 4:46 PM EDT on firstcoastnews.com

I am missing a very good friend today. John TenBroeck died this morning after a wonderful life of sharing his love of running with others. Dr. John, as we called him, was a man who gave much to the running community of Jacksonville. Through his long affiliation with and leadership of the Jacksonville Track Club, his dedication to the Jeff Galloway Training program and his love of people, he always had a smile and a bit of advice for all of us.

John was instrumental in our Inaugural 26.2 with Donna The National Marathon to Fight Breast Cancer. He took pride in getting new runners jazzed about marathoning. Even when cancer made it hard for him to run, John didn't stop. He just kept smiling and coached our walkers. He called them "The Lovers". His reason? "We're out here so long we must love it!" That was John. He couldn't wait to give us a joke, albeit a twisted one, before most of our Saturday training runs.

Even in his final days John was laughing. He was a huge Gator fan and loved to give me grief about my Seminoles. He would always make sure if I was rolling video on him during my running journals to insert a rousing 'Go Gators!' just to get to me.

I asked John one day recently if he was ready if it was his time to go. He told me he was going to do all he could to live, but felt just fine about the next life too. So when people say John "lost his battle with cancer" I know they mean well. But those words are a disservice to this great man. We are all going to die from something. The winning or losing is in the way we live. It's how John lived that was his victory and one he graciously shared with all of us.

*　　*　　*

My blog posted, I finish my lead- in script to the on-air story and head for the set. My news director Mike Garber stops me before I get there. Mike has been training with us every Saturday since we started back in July in a group much faster than mine. He's been a big supporter of the race, and is planning to run the full marathon.

"Hey, tough news about Dr. John," he says. "I'm glad you're doing a story."

"Do you know how he got that name?"

"No, am I going to find out?"

"Only if you tune in to First Coast News at 5:30," I say, in my best news promotion voice.

"I'll do it."

At 5:30 I run my journal tribute, complete with Dawn's account of how John TenBroeck became Dr. John.

"It was 2002. We were at the Chicago Marathon and it was bitterly cold. We were all looking for extra clothes to put on and the only clothes John could talk anyone out of, were these doctor scrubs someone had. He was going to just wear them over his running shorts and singlet until he warmed up. But he had so much fun pretending to be a doctor that he kept them on the entire 26.2 miles. Every time we passed a beautiful woman he would offer to examine her. I lost him at about mile 12. As far as I know, he had no takers, but we started calling him Dr. John and he's been Dr. John ever since. He loved to make people laugh."

Classic.

29 | $\mathcal{H}$itting a High Note

Driving to a marathon planning meeting at the Dalton Agency. This is where my team holds most of its meetings these days. For a long time, I've been turning over an idea in my mind and I want to float it at today's gathering. On I-95, I pass a car with our running ribbon magnet stuck to the side. This still gives me such a thrill. I smile and wave at the person in the other car as I go by, and he looks at me a bit confused like 'what's up with this lady? But OK.' He waves back.

I'm in love with the world these days and if that occasionally makes me look a little trippy, so be it.

My phone rings and I can see from the area code it's my mother calling from Greenville, South Carolina.

I pick up and immediately start to sing.

"Happy Birthday to you, cha cha cha. Happy Birthday to you, cha cha cha, Happy Birthday dear Moootheeeer, Happy Birthday to You, cha cha chaaaaa!"

"Lovely my darling," she says. "You have the voice of an angel."

"You are a horrible liar, but thank you," I say.

"Thank *you* for the books!"

"Oh, you got them in time, good."

"Yes, and I'm looking forward to reading the larger one."

"Why not the other one?"

"Oh, I've already finished that one."

Elizabeth Barnett Hazouri is a voracious reader. She usually has at least three books going at once, so I can't miss by sending her books for a birthday present. Since my favorites are generally fiction, I have left it to Tim to share the 'God' books. Not this time, but it's taken me a while. I've certainly shared with her some of the things I'm learning. But if I'm Catholic, she's the pope. I'm not sure how these books will be received. In the spirit of love over fear, I finally decided to send them her way.

"So what do you think?"

"I think it's interesting, and certainly desirable to look at the world in a loving way," she says, offering me some positives.

Here comes the but.

"But I can't say it makes me feel particularly joyful."

My mother has struggled with depression for much of her life. She has a strong faith in God, but joyful would not be a word I would generally use to describe her. She is funny, and off the charts smart, but she has a hard time with the world. I've always teased her that she is the only woman alive who was born looking forward to dying and going to heaven.

"That's up to you, mom. You have to decide to feel joyful."

"Sometimes that's hard."

"Only if you decide it's hard. Mom I know you love God, but you are also one of the most fearful people I know. I come by it honestly."

"I don't know that I'm fearful," she says sounding more contemplative than hurt.

"By fearful, I mean by the definition in the book. You spend a lot of time down on yourself for not measuring up to what you think God expects of you."

"Well, I don't measure up. Not by a long shot."

"But if you constantly focus on not measuring up, how can you feel the love of God?"

She pauses. For a moment I think I've lost the connection.

"My sister Evelyn knows all about the joy," she says. "We've talked about it. I feel it sometimes but it's fleeting."

"OK, I have something I want you to try. Put in one of daddy's CDs. Find a song with a high C in it, and crank it. Tell me what you feel when you hear it."

I have been doing this quite spontaneously for months. My father was an opera singer. Amazing tenor voice. He died almost 20 years ago, and I miss him terribly. At least I did until all of this. After he was gone, I'd almost never listen to his music. It made me ache for him so badly. I loved hearing his voice, but could manage it only about once a year. It simply made me too sad.

"You've been listening to your father?"

"All the time. And to all the operas he loved. That high C. That's joy."

"OK, I'll try it. It hasn't made you sad?"

"Actually, it's been so beautiful mom. I've hooked on to this whole idea that time isn't linear. That everything exists at once, and so daddy exists now right here with me. I turn on his music and I just feel him. Do I still wish I could hug him? Sure. I miss his skin, but all the best parts are with me all the time now. It doesn't make me sad at all."

"Well, that's a miracle," she says with authority.

"It all is."

I've been circling the block around Hemming Plaza, not wanting to end the conversation in midstream. Now I'm late. This will surprise no one.

"Listen, I have to run into a meeting. You have a wonderful birthday and I'll talk with you soon, OK?

"OK, just remember what I always tell you."

"I know, Mom, Katie Couric calls her mother every day."

She read this in a magazine somewhere years ago and I never hear the end of it.

"You are the queen of Catholic guilt, do you know that?"

"Yes, and I'm not giving that up, no matter what your books say."

"Deal. I love you Mom."

"Love you too, darling. I'm off to find your father's music."

I pull my car into a spot on Laura Street, feed the meter, and walk the two blocks north to the Dalton Agency. The receptionist hits the buzzer that allows me to enter the main floor. The environment here is filled with my kind of energy. The walls are deep orange and they are covered with colorful ads the agency has produced.

The room we are meeting in is downstairs. There's a long mahogany table and the walls are made of eraser boards, which makes for quick work when we are making lists or brainstorming ideas.

"Good morning kids," I say. I call everyone a kid, even if they are older than me.

'Good mornings' come back to me from around the table. It's a packed room. There is Doug Alred, our course director, his wife Jane our expo manager, Val Brown, our sponsorship guru, Tiffany Davis, our logistics coordinator. Jim Dalton, who owns the agency, Melissa Loffelholz, our account manager here, Amanda Mousa, our media specialist, Sarah Horn from the city's Special Events Office, Susie Slappey our treasurer, Amanda Napolitano, who leads our Galloway group and heads up our website through her company, IDEA, and of course Jim Gilmore, aka Superman.

"Full house," I say. "Are we missing anyone?"

"Michael (Munz) is hoping to make it but he's running late from another meeting."

Of course.

Michael and I usually compete to see who can be latest to arrive.

"Would you like to run the meeting today Donna?" Jim asks.

Jim already knows the answer to this, but he's asking to be polite. I don't like to officially run the meetings because I will go off on my own tangents. Well I'll do that anyway, but I'd just as soon someone else kept us on course.

"Let Tiff do it," I say. "Otherwise, we'll be here for hours."

Tiffany is a petite African American woman with a wonderful knack for special events. She is not a runner, but she's a fast learner and she plays well with others. She is the anti-me when it comes to stating her opinion. She's the tactful one.

"OK, first item, merchandise," she says, reading from her notes.

She reaches under the table and pulls an army green t-shirt out of her big pink bag.

"Our logo is on the front," she says, showing the shirt around the room

"And on the back," she says, turning it over, "a big target, and the words COMBAT BREAST CANCER."

I'm already shaking my head.

"We had a lot of these green shirts left over from an order last year and I thought…"

"Nope, no, no, no."

I cut her off in mid-sentence.

The entire table turns to look at me.

"No fighting, no battle, no combat. No," I say.

I was going to wait to bring this up until all of the other agenda items were done, but Tiffany, much to her dismay, has presented me with the perfect opening.

"Listen, I've been thinking about this for a while. Dr. John's death and the whole 'losing his battle' thing was the clincher for me. I want to stop using all the fighting words," I say.

"You've all heard me allude to this before. I've got to stop practicing something I don't want to preach. Let's flip the way people view this whole breast cancer journey. Let's help women get healthier. If they are in a constant fighting mode, they are stressed. And stress causes illness."

I reach into a folder and pull out a study we reported on the news last week.

"This just came out. It's a new study from Israel. Four years, hundreds of women. Those who experienced two or more periods of extreme stress within a short amount of time had a 62 percent increase in their rates of breast cancer compared to those who did not go through those stressful periods. Folks this is not the only study out there. There are plenty of other findings that support me on this. I think it's important that we do our part to change the landscape."

"But everyone talks about the fight against breast cancer," says Amanda.

"Everyone but us. It has to start somewhere guys."

"Are you talking about actually changing the name of the race?" Jim asks.

"Eventually, yes but your copyright folks have told me that using your name is the best way to brand it. Even if we don't change it officially right now, we just start using different words."

"Our slogan is Finish Breast Cancer," Melissa says.

"Finish is fine," I say.

"Then let's go forward with that," says Sarah. "We'll just replace fight with finish on all of our materials and promotions."

"Good. Didn't mean to jump all over you, Tiff," I say, trying to soften my tone.

She raises both hands in the air in surrender.

"Hey, I'm not saying another word over here."

"No questions from you, Madame Treasurer?" I say, turning to Susie.

"I think you're going to cost me money with these changes, but that's fine," she says, looking up from the budget she has carefully planned and spread in front of her.

"Ah, the voice of reason," I say. "Always the wet blanket."

"I'm your girl," she says.

I have to mess with Sue. Another friend since childhood, she has always been the numbers girl. I don't do numbers. My pat line is that I got into broadcasting because I was told there would be no math.

We hit the rest of the agenda items: registration, race bags, medal orders, which ads are bringing us the most hits to our website.

"Runnersworld.com is our top referring site," says Amanda.

"Speaking of," Jim says, "your new ad in the magazine should be hitting any day."

"I know. I'm excited. Thanks for all your help on that."

"That's what we're here for," he says.

Jim doesn't charge us a cent for his creative team. He loves what we're doing and does all of his work pro-bono.

I look at my watch. I've got to get back to the house to get ready for work.

"OK, kids, I'm outa' here. Thanks for the time,"

I say my goodbyes and I walk out into the warmth of the early afternoon sun. Back in my car I take a deep breath and slip dad's CD into my player.

"Hello daddy," I say, as the first strains of his voice reach my ears. His high C brings him to the seat right next to me and I enjoy his company all the way home.

30 | Believing is Seeing

October 3, 2008

The wind chimes ring at my front door. Tim's in from his daily mail run.

"Mail man's here," he says. "And there's this hot blonde in the *Runner's World* magazine."

"Give it, give it, give it," I demand, reaching for the magazine.

Tim holds it beyond my reach.

"Patience, there running queen, I haven't even had a chance to get a good look yet myself."

"Hand it o-ver," I say. "I have been waiting to see this in print since July."

Tim lays the magazine on the table in front of me. There I am in the October issue of *Runner's World*, wearing our custom pink Oakley sunglasses with our running ribbon logo etched in one lens. Under the pictures it says Donna Deegan/ Breast Cancer Survivor/Runner.

This is surreal.

"I'm in freaking *Runner's World*," I scream.

I am practically dancing next to the table.

"How many years have you been wearing those pink glasses?"

"I don't know, a long time. To have Oakley agree to partner with us was huge. This is like a dream," I say pointing to the page.

"Well it sort of was wasn't it? Didn't you come up with this while you were meditating?"

"That's right I did. Perhaps not one of my deepest moments, but it was a damn good idea wasn't it? I emailed our sponsorship director and she was on it that day."

To: Valerie Brown

Subject: Oakley Ad

Val,

On the Oakley deal. There is just so much we can do with custom Oakley glasses. It is instant credibility for our race. I don't know if we could pitch this to them, or we just do it ourselves.. BUT I was doing my morning meditating and my pink Oakley's were sitting in front of me . . .   I start thinking "rose colored glasses" as a title for my next book project . . . then it hit me! What if Oakley did an ad for us like they do for Lance.(or maybe Lance's Foundation does it.I don't know)It's a black and white picture . . .

I am wearing the glasses, (or since it would have to be a close up maybe some really hot young runner chick is wearing them?) ONLY the glasses are pink with our logo. The line says something like:

"See the World through Rose Colored Glasses" and then something like "Oakley and 26.2 with Donna . . . the Vision to Finish Breast Cancer." If they didn't want to do it we could. I really think this could be a great addition to our already awesome campaign. These glasses could be a huge money maker for us if we play our cards right and increase our "cool" factor with those who don't necessarily have a direct link to breast cancer.

Donna

To: Donna Deegan

From: Valerie Brown

Subject: Re: Oakley Ad

LOVE IT! Will wait a few more minutes for him to get going in CA, and call!

*   *   *

"If meditation never did another thing for me, that would be enough," I say, enjoying the memory.

"And I love what the Dalton Agency did with your slogan."

"I really do too. Jim Dalton came up with it himself. When he first sent me the change, I was initially sort of irritated that he'd altered my line. The more I looked at it, though, the more I realized it was perfect. Replacing "see" with "save." It brings our mission home."

"*Save the World Through Rose Colored Glasses.* Brilliant!"

"I'll bet these things fly off the shelves," Tim says.

"They should bring in a lot of money for the cause," I say. "Mike Sterner, the guy from Oakley apparently has some people with strong ties to breast cancer in his family and Val says he really gets it. I need to call her. She's done a great job getting this whole deal done."

"How did Val find him?"

"Christina Langston over at Special Events. Apparently Mike and her husband are good friends. You give Val a name to work with and she's magic. Edith will have so much money for her research next year she won't know what to do with it all."

Tim reaches for my Oakley's on the table and holds them up to the light.

"Are you still thinking of using the rose colored glasses thing for the title of your book?"

"What book? I'm not even definite about writing it."

"Why not? You have so much you could share with people."

I wave my hand like I'm swatting a bug.

"First off, I'm not sure I can write about the cancer again. Even if I have some really positive things to share, I'm not sure I want to relive that part of my life. I don't know if that's healthy. Second of all, people might just think I'm a little nuts."

Tim raises his eyebrows and looks at me with a smile that's all lips.

"Don't even say it. I left myself completely open. I'm serious though. Think about my job, I'm a news anchor. It's one thing to be Catholic in the Bible belt. But a Catholic who meditates and does yoga? Some people are going to think I'm the anti-Christ."

"What happened to love over fear?"

His eyes are wide. His tone, incredulous.

"Don't give me that. You know what I mean, Tim. You get the emails just like me. We live in a very conservative area. Even in our own religion there are people who would cringe."

"So you shine a light there. That's all fear, Donna. This has increased your faith. Maybe you could pass that on to someone else."

"Who am I to be a teacher?"

"We're all teachers for each other, isn't that what Dr. Jampolsky says?"

He's so good at this. Pow, right where I live.

I smile and shake my head.

"OK, Smarty, do you always have to learn more than me? What if I just want to be the 'hot blonde' in the *Runner's World* magazine?"

Tim returns the smile.

"You're going to be impossible to live with now, aren't you?"

"Does that insinuate I wasn't already?" I move close to him and give him a gentle kiss.

He wraps his arms around me and pulls me to him.

"What do I get for putting up with you?"

I look into his eyes and bring my lips to within an inch of his.

"I can probably score you a pair of custom pink Oakley's." I breathe the words.

"Well, that's not exactly what I had in mind," he whispers into my ear, "but we can negotiate."

I take Tim's hand and lead him off toward the bedroom.

"Don't think I won't wear them," he says. "I'm completely secure in my manhood."

"You'll have to prove it," I say, closing the door behind us.

31 | Conversation with God

Morning's first light is streaming through my window. Tim's already been up for an hour. I push the button on my watch that illuminates the time. 6:24. Need to get up at 6:30 to take Danielle to school, but I wait for my personal wake up call. Tim always comes to my side of the bed and wakes me with a kiss and hug and an 'I love you' to start the day. Most mornings I'm still out cold when he arrives at 6:30 on the dot, but even on those rare days when I awaken early, unless nature deems otherwise, I wait for my morning kiss. It sets my day in motion exactly as I like it to begin. Start with love, let that be my intention for the day. Closing my eyes, I begin my daily gratitude list.

Thank you for my perfect health.

Thank you for my wonderful husband.

Thank you for my beautiful children.

Thank you for everyone you have placed in my path to bring me to your perfect peace and joy.

Then my mantra.

I am whole.

I am happy.

I am healthy.

I am life.

I am love.

I am harmonious.

I am abundant in all good things.

Let it all settle into me as I once again envision God's perfect white light sweeping through every cell of my body.

There's a feeling of peace that even I find surprising. Today I'll have blood work at Mayo and then a PET scan. Edith has decided I need the scan every three months now. This will be my third since ending chemo back in April. Upon reading each one, she's proclaimed them "beautiful." Same with my blood markers, which have dropped steadily since mid-summer. After today's scan I'll tell her I want to stretch them out a bit.

I take a moment to picture Edith in my mind. She gets up from her desk, throws her arms wide open and tells me exactly what I want to hear.

"Donna, this is fantastic!" Fantastic is one of Edith's favorite words. Then she once again proclaims my results "beautiful," tells me to have a nice life and sends me on my way.

I run over this movie in my head a number of times and it makes me smile. I'm already feeling grateful for test results I have not yet received.

It is no small point that I'm thinking this way. In the past I wouldn't even allow myself to consider such a thing until after the results came in. I would've worried that I'd "jinx" things by being too optimistic. One day last winter, I actually asked Edith to start giving me a sedative before my PET scans because I simply could not quiet the fearful voices in my head.

I'd toss and turn the night before. Lay awake and ruminate on the past and worry over the future. Tim had to be with me every moment or I couldn't deal. This way of thinking has evaporated like sweat on a cool day.

My last PET scan three months ago, Tim had a weather presentation planned at one of the area schools. He's been doing this once a week for as many years as I can remember. He offered to postpone it, but I told him I'd be fine. We were both a little stunned at the reversal, but I actually went by myself and fell asleep inside the scanner. That alone I consider a miracle.

Lying in bed this morning, I'm mindful of the fact the race is getting close. There have been some stressful moments in the past few weeks. One of our sponsors was in, then out, then in again. One of the managers at an area hotel felt he wasn't getting his fair share of the marathon room nights and was threatening to take legal action.

Then there were the medals. Had we ordered enough? I have a week to decide whether to order more. The last thing I want is for some seven hour marathoner, to whom the medal means more than it does to any elite runner, to cross the finish line and be handed a card that says 'sorry, we ran out, your medal will be mailed to you.' These are the small details of a race that go with the territory, but details that can consume great gobs of time and energy.

Consequently, I have not been as consistent with my daily hour of meditation lately as I should be. I wonder briefly if this will cost me in the scanner, but I let the thoughts fall away as soon as they come. This type of thinking, I've learned, is based in fear and doesn't serve me. To focus there would only bring more fearful thoughts and there I am again, a hamster running the wheel.

I reach for *Love Is Letting Go of Fear* on my nightstand and turn to the lesson of the day. *The Past Is Over, It Can Touch Me Not.* It's illustrated by a smiling man walking in a sunny field next to a sign that says "The Present." He is tossing aside an old tape machine filled with pictures of the past and the future.

Perfect.

It's 6:30. As if on cue, the door opens and Tim sweeps me up in his arms and I'm ready for the day.

The smell of our morning French Roast tempts me toward the coffee pot but I pass it by. Nothing for me until after the scan.

Instead it's down the hall to wake up Drew who, now just weeks from turning 14, appears to take up his entire bed. He never seems to end up even remotely close to where he started out the night before.

"Time to get up, Drew, can I start the shower for you?"

As happens most days it takes three or four tries before I get any sign of life, much less an answer.

Finally, a grunt that I take for a yes, and I start out the door to the bathroom.

"Mom can you put my school clothes in the dryer?"

Ah, he is alive!

"Sure son, now hop in the shower."

"I will."

'I will'. If I could remove only two words from my son's vocabulary those would be the two. It is the answer he gives 95 percent of the time when asked to complete any task. He lifts the word "will" as if it weighs a thousand pounds. What it really means is 'not now'.

Drew has no less than five pairs of school uniform pants. Yet for some reason he must wear the same pair every day. He waits to put them in the washer until just before bed time and that leaves them for me to place in the dryer when I get him up. This is all part of our comfortable morning ritual.

I pad down the hallway to the kitchen, drop Danielle's bagel in the toaster and settle in to check the race email before it's time to leave for school. There's nothing pressing. A question about whether strollers will be allowed in the race (No). A couple of people ordered our custom pink Oakley's and they want to know when to expect delivery. I forward those on to Michelle Jacobs who runs our store. Another company wants to sell me finisher shirts. Nope, nothing's on fire. Good.

I look up to see Danielle hovering over my computer.

"Mom, can we go?"

"Yes, of course, just let me find my keys."

This takes me another five minutes to Danielle's great dismay. Finally I fish them out of my way too big excuse for a purse and we are ready.

I turn to Tim. "See you at Mayo in about an hour."

"Yep, I'm just going to drop off Drew, take a short run, hop in the shower and I'm heading your way."

I grab a quick kiss, tap on the bathroom door to remind Drew to call me on his way to school and we are off.

Danielle is actually old enough to drive herself now, but I insisted on one more year of taking her into Bishop Kenny. She just got her license in October, and it's a long drive from the beach. Plus I just can't bring myself to give up the time yet. Every morning I have her all to myself, captive in the car for 40 minutes. I cherish that time knowing full well how quickly it will pass.

"So you have your tests today," Danielle says, as we make our way down Beach Boulevard on our way to Kenny.

"Yes, every three months these days. I'm feeling really good about it."

"That's good. I'm sure they'll be great. I'll be thinking about you."

"Thank you sweetie."

"So what've you got today?"

"World History quiz, religion test, that's about it."

"You good to go on those?"

"Yep."

Our conversation becomes magically mundane and I soak in every word.

When we arrive at Bishop Kenny I drop her off close to her A mod (but not too close, that would be embarrassing).

"Bye Mom, love you," she says, hugging me.

"Love you too, Yellie."

And she disappears into the very same building where I attended classes 30 years ago.

On my way back to the beach, my phone rings and Drew checks in. It is 7:47. He has to be in his seat at St. Paul's Catholic School at 7:50.

"Cutting it a little close today, buddy?"

"I couldn't find socks," he says, with a yawn.

Drew always has a reason for his lateness. I'm the very last person who can criticize him on this front . Always trying to fit ten pounds of day into a five pound sack.

"I have pitching practice tonight," he reminds me.

"Got it. Anything else?"

"Vocab test."

"Are you ready?"

"I think so."

I hear the car door open.

"Do your socks match?"

"Probably not, but close enough."

"OK, buddy have a good day. I love you."

"Luh-ya-too- bye."

Drew runs the words together as if they are one word, barely distinguishable, but I'll take it. At his age saying I love you to your mom is probably not at the top of the cool things to do list.

Morning ritual complete, I make the turn onto I-95 South. That will connect me to J. Turner Butler Boulevard east to San Pablo Road and the Mayo Clinic (better known these days as the start line).

At the entrance to the clinic campus, long marathon banners featuring Kurtis' poster art announce the coming race. I smile, imagining the thousands of runners who will be here in February jogging nervously, checking their watches. The temperature this morning is in the upper 40's. Cool with some clouds. Not a bad day for a marathon, if the runners were here today.

Turning into the always crowded parking lot B, there's a space for me right in front.

This is exactly how my day is going to go.

I skip up the stairs to the exact spot where just months earlier I presented Mayo with the first ever check for breast cancer research generated from the marathon. A quick right takes me into the familiar morning buzz of the Davis Building cafeteria and then into the line for my blood work.

Mike is his regular one stick wonder self (God love that man!) and I am on my way upstairs for the scan. It takes about an hour of prep before I can actually get into the machine. First the injection of radioactive glucose. For the 24 hours leading up to my test I've been asked to consume no simple carbohydrates. They want my blood sugar to be fairly low when they begin the injection. The reason for this is that if cancer cells were present, they would uptake the glucose more quickly than normal cells, given that they have a higher metabolic rate. Those cells would be the only ones illuminated in the scan. The goal is no light bulbs.

Tim will be here shortly, but there is really no need for him to be here this early. I'm not supposed to talk for the hour I have to wait after my injection. I'm also asked to lie down in a separate room, lights out.

"We'll get you all set and you can get some sleep until it's time," the nurse says.

I used to find this suggestion utterly ridiculous.

Right! I'm sitting here about to wet my pants and you want me to sleep?

There were many such scans when tears would roll uninvited from my eyes just at the suggestion that I relax. This always embarrassed me.

Put on your big girl panties and deal with it.

I felt helpless, pathetic really but I couldn't control the tears.

Not today.

It did make me a tad nervous that it took the nurses three tries to get the needle into my vein.

"Third time's the charm," I told the last of three nurses who came at me with the silver point. "If you don't make it this time there won't be a fourth."

No offense meant, but I was already of the opinion that my earlier "beautiful pictures" were enough and that this was beginning to be radiation overload on my body. I trust Edith, and I know she just wants to stay on top of things, but PET scans carry many times the level of radiation that comes with an x-ray or even a CT scan and I'm not anxious to continue them on such a regular basis. Perhaps this was a sign that I just wasn't supposed to be here.

As it turned out the third time was in fact the charm and the debate in my head was done. I would approach the subject of subsequent tests with Edith later today.

Five minutes after the injection, I hear Tim come through the door in the next room. He peeks around the corner and I wave him over. He simply plants a kiss on my forehead and knowing I am not supposed to speak or have visitors he squeezes my hand and retreats to the waiting area. They will call him when it's time for the scan and he can sit with me then.

Five minutes after that, I am asleep.

In what seems like an instant the nurse is summoning me to the scan room. Tim follows right behind me.

Hop up on the narrow white bed and the tech straps me in. The straight jacket makes my heartbeat quicken. She places a cloth over my eyes so that the closeness of the scanner won't make me uneasy.

"You'll only be completely under there for about 20 minutes," she reassures me. "After that your head will be out and it will be another 20 to 25 minutes for the rest of your body."

"Thank you," I say, then turn my attention to Tim.

"Want to read to me?"

"Sure."

He pulls from his backpack my copy of *The Holy Longing* and begins to read one of my favorite chapters.

I'm barely able to make out the words inside the machine but I hear his voice. That's all I really need. Tim's voice humming steadily in my ears, covering me like a blanket.

The pages are so familiar to me now. I almost know them by heart. The author is describing how Jesus saw God the Father as a relaxed, loving God.

"To understand Jesus' attitude and his teachings, it can be helpful to imagine that through his entire lifetime, God, his Father, kept whispering in his ears that blessing from his baptism: "You are my beloved son, and in you I am well-pleased. … Thus when Jesus looks at the poor, the hungry, and the weeping and sees them as blessed, it is because first of all he is hearing God's voice inside of himself, telling him that God is seeing him and the world in that way.

The machine clicks and my body inches slowly out of the scanner. I can see light through the cloth that covers my eyes so I know my head is now beyond the dark confines of the tube.

Tim continues to read.

"There is a contemporary Buddhist parable that can help us to understand what is being said here: One day the Buddha, badly overweight, was sitting under a tree. A young soldier, trim and handsome, came along, looked at the Buddha and said 'You look like a pig!' The Buddha replied 'Well you look like God!' 'Why would you say that?' asked the rather surprised soldier. 'Well,' replied the Buddha, 'we see what's inside us. I think about God all day and when I look out that is what I see. You, obviously, must think about other things…"

I realize that I've really come to believe this is true. We see what we choose to see. We can view the world through loving eyes and therefore we will see our circumstances and those around us as loving, God's perfect creation. If we choose to look through eyes of fear, we cannot help but see others and ourselves in a more negative light, always expecting the worst of both.

"Click, click, click." The scanner continues its work.

Tim is still reading when the tech's voice breaks in. It's the part of the book that finally solved the mystery of Dan Brown's inscription in my book.

"Only a couple of more minutes and we should be all done," the tech says.

Already? Wow!

"*... in Rembrandt's painting of the Prodigal son, the figure painted there, representing God, has a number of interesting features: First of all, he is depicted as blind. His eyes are shut, and he sees the prodigal son not with his eyes but with his heart (to which he is tenderly holding his son's head). The implication is obvious, God sees with the heart. Moreover, the figure representing God has one male hand (which is pulling the wayward son to himself) and one female hand (which is caressing the son's back). Thus God is presented here as both mother and father, loving as does a woman and does a man.*"

Moments later I'm unstrapped from the table and a nurse comes in to tell me I'm free to go.

Tim and I stop into the cafeteria for my long delayed morning cup of coffee. I take it to go, anxious to get back out into the sunlight.

"You did great in there today," he says.

"Well, having you there with me helps tremendously, but yes what a different world for me than just a few months ago. No panic at all."

"That must feel like a nice affirmation."

"It does. It's such a relief to let go of the fear. Now, I only need one thing," I say with great sincerity.

"Yes?"

"Food! I'm starving!"

"I'm with you there. Remember we are meeting mom and dad for lunch at Harry's Seafood before our appointment with Edith," he says.

"OK, why don't we meet up at home first and we'll just walk over."

"See you there, Mi Amore," he says. "I was proud of you today."

"Thanks, Sweetheart."

I reach my car, slip into the driver's seat and close the door.

Suddenly I'm overcome with a sense of gratitude for the grace I've received on this day. Not only did I not fall apart, I was peaceful. Truly peaceful.

I recall my concern from the morning. Had my months of meditation prepared me for this? Even given the craziness of the last several weeks?

I lay my head back on the seat and smile.

"Thank you for not abandoning me," I say aloud to myself.

Immediately an answer comes back, as loud and as clear as if someone were sitting in the car having a conversation with me.

"I could never abandon you. Only you can abandon me."

I am momentarily stunned. I wasn't expecting or looking for an answer. At least I don't think so.

"Thank you," is all I can muster. "Thank you so much."

Two hours later, we have stuffed ourselves at Harry's and we're on our way back to see Edith.

"Mind if we stop and grab a cup of coffee on the way?" Tim asks.

It's been a full morning, and I've filled him in on my "conversation" in the car. We are both giddy, but wiped out.

"Of course."

We stop at a little drive through called "Cuppy's". The sign has a face on the front that looks sort of like one of those little packman creatures from the old video game. Tim orders the coffee and the man hands the steaming cups through the window. On top of the drinking hole in each lid there is a stick-on daisy. A little cover to keep the coffee from spilling until you're ready to drink it. I peel mine off and paste it to my cheek.

"What do you think?"

"Very festive," Tim says, with an approving nod.

We park at Mayo, take the elevator to the 8th floor and are taken directly to an examining room to wait for Edith. The nurse flips on a green light at the door to let Edith know we are waiting. I am so excited I can hardly wait to see her. I've been in this room and others like it a thousand times. Today it seems friendlier somehow.

"Hello, dear friends," Edith says bounding into the room.

"Hello, Edith!" I almost sing the words.

"My you are in good spirits today. I love the flower on the cheek. Nice touch. But I haven't even told you your results yet."

"Would you like for me to tell you my results?"

"That won't be necessary. I have them right here," she says, practically singing back at me.

"Donna, this is fantastic. Your scan is beautiful and your marker number is perfect. Just where we want it to be."

My grin is so wide it might split my face.

"At some point you are going to ask me what I'm doing and we are going to get all of your other patients doing it," I say.

"I would love to hear about what you're doing. But whatever it is, keep doing it, eh?"

32 | *V*iew From Love

February 15, 2009

I grab the morning paper from the mat at the front door and take a moment to survey the weather.

"It's not raining anymore," I yell back at Tim.

"Thank you, Donna," he says in a sing-songy voice that lets me know he is well aware of what the weather is or isn't doing.

I walk back into the kitchen, set the paper on the counter.

"I think it's going to be a beautiful day," I say.

"It's going to be a beautiful day, no matter what, but I wish you wouldn't get your hopes up," Tim says.

He is standing over his weather maps, staring at blobs of color on the radar.

"I'm just saying, I think we're going to see some blue out there today," I say. "Your competition might agree with me."

"Oh, now you're hurting me. Since when do you watch the competition?"

"Since Mike agreed to let me do the interview on channel 4's morning show this year, God bless his heart, I had a chance to watch John's forecast. He said we could get a dry window during the race."

"I said that, too. You could get a dry window. I just said it's not going to be a blue window and the rest is very much on the edge. Donna look, I've been trying to be optimistic for you all week, but darlin' we are going to be lucky if we make it to the start line today without a torrential downpour. There is not going to be any blue. Well, I take that back. Ninety percent of me says, no way. Ten percent says, if your angels show up all bets are off."

"I heard you say that on the air last night."

"I did. Listen, I want to believe too, but…"

"But you don't see it happening."

"I'm just looking at what's right in front on me, Donna and I want you to appreciate it if we can just stay dry until after the start of the race. That would be blessing enough."

"I hear you. I still think we're going to see some blue. Susan's got my back on the weather. I don't care what your maps say."

"Would you like to take a look for yourself?"

"No, I would not."

I pick up my pink sunglasses and place them dramatically on the top of my head.

"I fully expect to use these today," I say, raising an eyebrow to my husband.

I return my attention to the paper, thumbing through it for news about the marathon.

"Mark Woods wrote his column about us today," I say, pulling the Metro section from the rest.

"The Headline says *26.2 With Donna Defies the Economy.*"

"Well, you've got to like that."

I like the way Mark says just about anything. He's a talented writer. He's an almost equally talented runner. Mark was one of the first local people I went to for advice when I made the decision to create this marathon. Many of the special, runner friendly, touches on the course are based on his observations as a runner.

"I think Mark is going to try to break 85 minutes in the half today," Tim says.

"That fast? That's great. Want me to read you the column? It's pretty cool. It's all about the reach of the race. The draw of the marathon plus the cause. He talked with two girls who came all the way from Alaska and brought their entire families."

"We need to get going if we're going to beat the traffic. You can read it to me on the way."

We gather our gear and head for the start line at the Mayo Clinic.

Joan Benoit Samuelson, who has become a dear friend over the past year, meets me at the staging area for the elite athletes. She will once again, lead the women's field in the half marathon. After last year's race she went on to reach her goal of a sub 2:50 finishing time in the Boston Marathon.

"Your race really inspired me for Boston," she told me during a subsequent visit to her home in Maine. "I mean you see all the survivors and what they've been through, and what they've been able to accomplish and then you think you're having a bad hair day? I don't think so."

Joanie has been a huge supporter in our efforts to grow the race. It's great to see her back at starting line.

"I still say the half marathon is a much nicer distance," she says, still doing her best to convince me. "But I'm going to come out and run you in the last couple of miles, OK?"

"I will look forward to that Joanie. Just think slooow."

Joanie had toyed with running the full distance with me, but I persuaded her to run her own race. I would just put too much pressure on myself to speed up. Tim went out for a "casual warm up run" with her the day she came to town and it almost killed him. He loved it.

"I just kept telling myself, you're running with Joanie Benoit, you can not pass out," he told me later. He has told that story to everyone who will listen in the past two days.

I glance up at the sky. No sun in sight. Joanie's looking too.

"What do you think about the chance of rain Tim?" she says.

"The rain's going to hold off," I interject. "I suspect we might even see some sun."

"She's the meteorologist today," Tim says. "We're not going with science."

"Well that works," she says.

Joanie gives me a conspiratorial wink.

"OK you two, have a good run," she says, with a thumbs up.

"You too, Joanie."

She takes her place with the other elites and the countdown begins.

"5,4,3,2,1."

The cannon sounds, and pink confetti fills the air for our second annual race. I pat my button, with Susan's radiant face, that is once again pinned to my shirt, and brush my fingers over the top of the symbol around my neck. My friend, Joni Fausett gave me the necklace last year as I was recovering from surgery. It's a simple red string with a small silver circle in the middle. In Chinese it says "healing." It has come to represent what this journey is all about for me.

We cross the J. Turner Butler Bridge and just like last year the chopper buzzes overhead. The sky is saturated in gray. But it only serves to bring out the colors on the course. Shades of pink are everywhere. Pink polka dots, pink knee socks, pink wigs.

"Go, Spidey Go!"

People are laughing and pointing. A man in a pink Spiderman costume runs by shooting imaginary webs from his fingertips.

Full body tights?

"That's gonna be hot at mile 22," Tim says, shaking his head.

"Hey look, it's the Alaska girls! They're wearing the shirts Mark was talking about in the article."

'Wild Salmon Run And So Do We' is printed on the back with pictures of the pink fish sprinting.

You gotta love runners.

We pass the first water stop.

"Active Water here!" screams a volunteer at the table.

I grab the sports drink from her outstretched arm, down it, and we round the ramp for Jacksonville Beach.

The man who owns Active Water, Doug MacLean, is one of the thousands of stories out here today. This is his 80th marathon. He's running with his son Hunter. Both are looking to finish the marathon in around three hours, with Hunter actually hoping to break three. In addition to sponsoring the race, they flew all the way from Seattle to run it.

At 16th Avenue South I can see the entrance to the Memorial Mile. It's the portion of our race where we run directly onto the sand and this year we've marked the spot as a tribute to those we've lost and a promise to those still here. Large flags resembling sails flutter in the wind.

"Oh, Donna," Tim says, choking up.

There amid the flags is a 20 foot tall banner of Dr. John TenBroeck. The picture of him is in full stride with a caption proclaiming "DR. JOHN WE LOVE YOU AND WE MISS YOU" along with John's favorite call at the start of a run. "It's a beautiful day to live and run in Jacksonville!"

I didn't tell anyone about the banner except for Doug Alred, our course director, and Tiffany Davis, our logistics coordinator. I wanted it to be a surprise.

"Another one of my angels now," I say to Tim.

We turn north onto the sand where we are met by huge sandwich boards with words like hope and faith and believe.

"I signed the one that says believe," I say, pointing to the third board in front of us.

There are ten of them in all, and thousands of messages joining mine. We had the boards up for runners to sign at the expo, and they were placed on the beach just before dawn. Now people are racing up to them, touching the names they added, taking pictures.

I take a deep drag on the salt air and scan the ocean. My heart skips a beat. *Am I seeing this?*

To the northeast, a pod of dolphins is literally just yards offshore. One of them jumps so high it almost clears the water. I tap Tim's arm, not wanting to take my eyes off the spot.

"Tim, did you see that?"

He doesn't answer.

"Hey," I say again, finally turning to see why he isn't responding.

But Tim isn't looking at the ocean. He is running with his eyes locked on the sky. Not the whole sky, but a very tiny clear patch of pure blue. I break into a goofy grin and start to giggle.

"Well, who needs science when you've got angels," Tim says.

"Good morning Susan," I sing, as if the words were music.

By the time we exit the sand two miles later, the small patch has spread as far as we can see in front of us. The entire sky is a bright clear blue.

I grab my rose colored glasses from the top of my head and put them on.

"Glad I have these," I say.

The view is spectacular.

$\mathcal{E}$pilogue: Dragonfly

June 23, 2009

"Tim, I had the weirdest experience last night," I say, as we sip our morning coffee in the kitchen.

"I was meditating and I fell asleep, or not. I don't know. This is what I remember. I am standing in a small room. I'm guessing some sort of break room, though none I've been in before. Dee Dee Lang is there, of all people."

"Your first director at the TV station?"

"Yes, 20 years ago!"

"OK," he says, and I can see he's about to say something else.

"Let me just get through this, because I don't want to forget anything. We are looking at a mess on the counter. Half eaten snacks and remnants of meals are everywhere. There's this crumbled pile of graham crackers and chocolate on the counter, so I say 'Why don't I clean this up?' She says 'No, you should leave that. I think someone may be coming back for it.'"

"Then I see this half sandwich left behind on the counter, and I say 'OK, but I think I could throw this out don't you?' But as I get closer I notice there are two dragonflies sitting on top of the sandwich and I comment on how odd that is. Just then, one of the dragonflies takes off and lands on the back of my neck, inside my shirt. I wake up, or come out of my meditation with my hands down the back of my shirt, trying to reach the dragonfly."

"Seemed pretty real, huh?" Tim says.

"So real, that I couldn't get it out of my head. So I go to my computer and google 'dreaming of dragonflies.' And this is the first site that comes up."

I motion Tim over to my computer and show him the web page.

"Look at this. It says dreaming of dragonflies often means that unseen help or a spiritual message is available to you. It says it may be calling me to change habits that don't serve me and to a realization that I am creating all that is in front of me."

Tim smiles.

"I know, I'm a freak," I say. Am I just getting weirder and weirder or what?"

"Well, if you are, you're my kind of weird. I think this is just more affirmation of everything you're doing. I think you are in a really great place to hear right now."

"But I've been doing that. I've made so many changes, found so many wonderful teachers. What am I missing?"

"It's all a journey isn't it, Donna? Do any of us ever really get there? I think life's always a work in progress, don't you? You just need to stay aware of what's happening in front of you. Your answers will come."

"OK. It's just almost scary, that's all."

"Why is it scary? I think it's exciting."

"It's exciting to you because you aren't afraid to be out there somewhere," I say, waving my arms in the air. "You are so comfortable with all of these different paths. And intellectually, while I can believe they all lead to the same place, it scares me to put myself too far out there. We've talked about that. This is pushing pretty hard on my Catholic school boundaries."

Tim points to a painting on the wall in front of us. "Remember your reaction when you first saw this?"

The painting is oil on canvas. I knew it was mine the moment I saw it. An artist by the name of Shannon Wing painted it. Her theme is water. Usually surfing. This piece is called "Take-Off". It shows a blonde woman with a pony tail and in a blue bathing suit presumably taking off on a wave. But to me, she just appears to be floating on a swirl of blue and white energy. There's light around her in shades of pale yellow and white. Beyond her light the sky is ablaze with hues of orange. We bought the painting shortly after my surgery. Before I started down my current path. Or at least before I was aware of it.

"It definitely spoke right to me," I say warming to the image.

"A part of you knew already where you wanted to go. Donna, all of these experiences, they are just different ways to remind yourself that God is with you. That if you open your heart and listen with it, you have nothing to fear. Come on, this is great stuff."

It's late morning now and I'm on my way to my weekly acupuncture appointment with Dr. Huo. My friend, Pat stops me on the way out of the condo's lobby. We chat for a few moments but there is this incessant buzzing sound behind us.

"What is that?" Pat asks.

We turn to see a dragonfly hovering next to the light on the ceiling.

"Oh we have to let it out," I say propping the front door open. "It won't survive in here."

Bob, our grounds supervisor comes in with a broom.

"Don't hurt it, Bob," I say.

"I'm not going to hurt it, Donna, I'm just going to give it a lift."

Bob holds out the broom and the dragonfly hops right on like it's hailing a cab or something.

He sticks the broom out the door and the dragonfly takes off.

I finish my conversation with Pat, and walk out to my car.

Immediately the dragonfly buzzes my shoulder. It flies around me all the way through the parking lot and to my car.

"You didn't tell me that was your pet, Donna," Bob says, laughing.

I laugh too, but this is getting stranger every minute.

"OK, buddy, I get it," I say, looking at my new friend. "I'm wide awake. Just tell me what I'm looking for. I've got to go now."

I get into my car and the dragonfly zooms off.

I'm replaying the whole thing in my mind as I wait in the treatment room for Dr. Huo. There is a tap on the door and a woman walks in. She has curly dark blonde hair that rests just above her shoulders. Part of it is pulled back off her face, highlighting her cheekbones and her dark brown eyes. She's wearing a white lab coat over a red blouse, and a skirt with flowers. I've seen her once before with Dr. Huo, but I don't know her.

She sees the confused look on my face.

"Dr. Huo's not here today," she says. "My name is Dr. Corrales, but please just call me Ducie, I'm his partner."

"Why isn't he here? Is he alright?"

She pauses for a moment apparently choosing her words.

"He isn't coming back. He has so much going on with his travels and his practice in Orlando. He's asked me to come instead."

I feel instantly insecure. Dr. Huo has been treating me for almost a full year now. I've come to depend on his energy. Tears prick the corners of my eyes and I do my best to wish them away.

"I'm so sorry," I say embarrassed by my inability to check my emotions.

"It's OK," she says, placing a hand on my shoulder. "Everyone's been a little emotional today."

"It's just that…"

"I know, you feel that Dr. Huo has been a big part of your healing, and he has. Dr. Huo has many gifts, Donna, but I have my own and I hope you allow me to share them with you."

Her voice is warm. Her eyes focused on mine.

"I just feel like he's left me at such a critical time." I say the words haltingly, not really wanting to go there.

"Why is that?"

I take a deep breath and lean forward. There is something about this woman that makes me want to share with her.

"Well, I had a spike in a blood marker a month or so ago. My doctor immediately wanted to do another PET scan, but I asked if we could just retest in a week or two. She agreed. I had been going through a major stressful few weeks at work, and Dr. Huo had been on vacation, so I hadn't seen him as much. I called him and asked if we could up my number of treatments until it was time for my next test. We did, and my numbers came back down. I have no idea whether one has to do with the other, but I guess what it comes down to is I just want to make sure I'm OK."

"And you're afraid without Dr. Huo you aren't OK?"

"I don't know. It goes against everything I've been practicing. My circumstances shouldn't determine my peace, but occasionally I still get stressed out about it all. Not crazy stressed like I used to, but more than I want. Part of it for me has to do with wanting to avoid those invasive tests. I'd prefer to put good things in my body. Radioactive glucose isn't high on my list of healthy favorites. But I'm sure that's not all of it."

"What does Dr. Huo say about all this?"

"Ironically, he says the same thing my oncologist says. That one blood test isn't significant. He says I'm fine and that I shouldn't worry. The thing is, I've been really good with that for the most part. Very peaceful. I guess this just shows me I still have a ways to go."

Her lips curve into a barely detectable smile. It's more her eyes that are smiling. She nods.

"Let's see what we've got going on here," she says.

She takes my pulses, closes her eyes and places her hands over me, but not on me. She moves them in the air just over my body. This goes on for several minutes. Dr. Huo never did this. I'm fascinated.

"Donna, may I tell you something?" she asks, finally opening her eyes. I nod.

"Dr. Huo is right. You're fine. You do not have the pulses of a person with cancer. There is no cancer in your body right now. Perhaps it's time for you to accept that you've graduated. You have only one ailment that I can see, and that's fear."

I'm not sure how to take this. The words are comforting if they are to be believed, but what does this tell me about myself? Have I failed at the one thing I've been working most to change?

"Well if that's the case, I'm not nearly as far down the right path as I thought," I say.

"Don't be hard on yourself. I would say you are 90 percent there. But 10 percent of you still doesn't want to let it go. The fear is your shield."

"My shield?"

"You think it protects you."

"From what?"

"The risk you take by totally giving yourself over to belief. Or I should say the perceived risk. You want it both ways. You want to believe, but you want to leave yourself an out. The problem is, believing something 90 percent of the time is not believing."

"I guess that's true," I confess, feeling somewhat deflated by the knowledge.

"Listen to me," she says, her body language urgent, "You can believe. And if anything ever presents itself that is not in line with what you know to be true, you must stay focused on the truth."

"The truth?"

"Donna, I am a healer. I'm an acupuncture doctor, but I will share with you that I'm also a Shaman. There are a number in my family going back many years. From the time I was a little girl I've known I'm also a seer. I was afraid to tell anyone for the longest time. I thought something was wrong with me. Finally I told my mother. It took her a while, but she eventually told me the whole story. The history of my family and my gift."

She takes my hand. Her words are slow and deliberate.

"You have a light in you that I can see very clearly. You are going to live to be a very old woman."

I'm stunned.

I've been saying those words to myself for a long time. Even picturing myself as an old woman going the same way my grandfather did. On the couch, reading a favorite book, laying my head back to take a nap and traveling seamlessly from this life to the next. But to hear someone else say them to me, someone I've just met is a shock.

She registers the look on my face.

"Don't make this more pressure on yourself, Donna. I'm not saying you are never going to face another challenge in your life, simply that you should rest in the knowledge that no matter what is ahead, it's going to be alright."

I've heard those words before. How much do I want to share with this woman? Am I reaching?

"Something you want to say?"

"Oh, a million things, but this is, all, well it's a little strange."

"Well, I've got to tell you in a way it is for me too. I don't usually just stroll into a new patient's room and spill all these things about myself. I don't see things about everyone. But what can I say? I call 'em like I see 'em and I can also see you are in a place to accept it."

Am I?

I don't answer immediately. A small part of me wants to jump off the table and step out onto the solid sidewalk, but a strong voice is telling me to let it be. Stay, push through the discomfort.

"I had this weird dream or something last night," I say exhaling. I tell her the whole story I shared earlier with Tim. "Here's the problem. I'm basically an old fashioned Catholic girl who's trying to see how all of this fits into my world."

She laughs. "It fits in perfectly."

She reaches into her shirt and pulls out a necklace. It's a crucifix. I can hardly believe my eyes.

"I'm just a Catholic girl too," she says. In fact my full name is Dulce Maria Corrales. That's about as Catholic as it gets."

"No way," I say.

"Way. I'm named after Mary."

"Sweet Mary, if I have my Spanish right."

"You do."

The tumblers start to click into place in my brain.

"Well in that event, and considering the fact that you probably won't think I'm crazy, I'll tell you my Mary story."

"I'd love to hear it."

I settle into the memory.

"It was after my second diagnosis. I was in the middle of a particularly tough round of chemo. Had really broken down. I stopped on the side of the road on the way home from work one night around midnight and just let loose on God. Literally begged for help. The next afternoon when I got back to the office, I had this message from a guy who had called at like four in the morning. His name was Jeff McCrory and he built all the Mary shrines for churches and businesses around the area that wanted them. I had never met him. He'd never met me. He was just a nice guy who had prayed to Mary for years asking her to let him know if there was ever anyone he could help."

"And she wanted him to help you?"

"That's what he said. We met up at one of his shrines. He wanted to tell me the story face to face and he said he had a gift for me. Jeff told me that Mary appeared at the foot of his bed just after four in the morning. I still remember his exact words. 'I'm telling you, Donna, I'm as sane as they get, and I know the difference between a dream and reality and this was no dream.'"

I smile at the memory of Jeff's face. Animated with excitement. Joyful.

"He said she didn't speak, but he knew immediately he was to call me with a message."

"Which was?"

"Everything will be alright."

I tear up again just saying the words.

"I've got chills," Ducie says.

"Me too. He gave me a scapular that I treasure to this day. And we still keep in touch occasionally. We share a love for the rosary. I think we both realize we connected on something very special. Do you ever say the rosary?"

"Every morning and sometimes at night."

I shake my head, and raise my palms in question.

"Well, Ducie, you are going to have to teach me how you got from point A to point Z on the Catholic comfort meter with all this."

"I'll do my best. I need to look in on a couple of other patients. I'll be back in a few minutes."

She places my needles and leaves me to my thoughts.

The moments tick by. My mind is working furiously trying to make sense of all this.

"Donna, can I come in?"

I prop myself up on my elbows. It's Frank Pirisino, one of the volunteers at The Wellness Center.

"I brought you something."

Frank hands me a beautiful wooden bracelet. Each piece of wood is connected by gold balls. And each has a picture on it. I turn it in my hand. There is the Virgin Mary, Jesus in various stages of life, and Padre Pio. I'm not sure whether to laugh or cry.

"Frank, this is beautiful."

"I had it blessed for you Donna. I thought you'd like it."

"I love it, thank you," I say, sliding the bracelet onto my wrist.

"I'll let you relax," he says and he's gone.

Ducie walks back in and makes a motion like she's been hit by a wave or something.

"Wow, you've got quite the energy going on in here. Your mind is working overtime to process all of this."

"You know, I hope you're not going to do that all the time," I say. "That's a little creepy. Hey, look what I've got," I say, holding my wrist up to show her the bracelet. "Frank gave it to me."

She looks at the pictures on each piece of wood and nods decisively as if she's just heard someone make a very good point.

"It's very beautiful," she says.

I look at her and take a deep breath. I can hardly believe I just met this woman. It's as if I've known her forever.

"What does all this mean, Ducie? Am I being led to something? And if so, what?"

"Donna, we're all being led to something. We just have to be aware of that fact. And to do that, each one of us has to use the tapes that are recorded in our own brains. My tapes are Catholic. So are yours. It's how we were raised. It's in our roots. It's what we believe. It doesn't make anyone else's path less true. We are all taking our own roads to get to the one God."

She points above her head.

"We can all be great teachers for each other. What you must ultimately realize though is that all of your teachers are just that, but they are not the answer."

"So what is the answer?"

"You are the answer. And all you have to do is ask yourself, what is the question."

My marathon continues.